INITIATION, HUMAN AND SOLAR

BOOKS BY ALICE A. BAILEY

Initiation, Human and Solar

By

ALICE A. BAILEY

LUCIS PUBLISHING COMPANY

New York

LUCIS PRESS LTD.

London

First Printing, 1922

Sixth Printing, 1972 (First Paperback Edition)

Seventeenth Printing, 1997

ISBN No. 0-85330-110-7

Library of Congress Catalog Card Number: 52-000179

The publication of this book is financed by the Tibetan Book Fund which is established for the perpetuation of the teachings of the Tibetan and Alice A. Bailey.

This Fund is controlled by the Lucis Trust, a tax-exempt, religious, educational corporation.

The Lucis Publishing Company is a non-profit organisation owned by the Lucis Trust. No royalties are paid on this book.

This title is also available in a
clothbound edition.

It has been translated into Armenian, Croatian, Danish, Dutch, French, German, Greek, Italian, Japanese, Polish, Portuguese, Romanian, Russian, Spanish Swedish and Yugoslavian. Translation into other languages is proceeding.

LUCIS PUBLISHING COMPANY
120 Wall Street
New York, NY 10005

LUCIS PRESS, LTD.
Suite 54
3 Whitehall Court
London SW1A 2EF

MANUFACTURED IN THE UNITED STATES OF AMERICA
By Fort Orange Press, Inc., Albany, NY

Dedicated with
reverence and gratitude
to
the Master K. H.

THE LORD BUDDHA HAS SAID

that we must not believe in a thing said merely because it is said; nor traditions because they have been handed down from antiquity; nor rumors, as such; nor writings by sages, because sages wrote them: nor fancies that we may suspect to have been inspired in us by a Deva (that is, in presumed spiritual inspiration) ; nor from inferences drawn from some haphazard assumption we may have made; nor because of what seems an analogical necessity; nor on the mere authority of our teachers or masters. But we are to believe when the writing, doctrine, or saying is corroborated by our own reason and consciousness. "For this," says he in concluding, "I taught you not to believe merely because you have heard, but when you believed of your consciousness, then to act accordingly and abundantly."

(Secret Doctrine, Vol. III, page 401.)

FOREWORD

The subject of Initiation is one that has a great fascination for thinkers of all schools of thought, and even those who remain sceptical and critical would like to believe that this ultimate attainment is possible. To those who do not believe that such a goal is possible this book is offered for what it may be worth as a formulation of an interesting hypothesis. To those who anticipate such a consummation of all their endeavours, this book is tendered in the hope that it may prove an inspiration and a help.

Among occidental thinkers at this time there is a wide diversity of view upon this momentous subject. There are those who think that it is not of sufficient immediate importance to engross their attention, and that if the average man adheres to the path of duty and high-minded attention to the business in hand, he will duly arrive at his destination. This is undoubtedly true, yet as capacity for increased service, and the development of powers to be used in the helping of the race are the reward of the man who is willing to make the increased effort and to pay the price which initiation demands, perhaps this book may spur some on to attainment who might otherwise have drifted slowly towards their goal. They will then become givers, and not the recipients of help.

There are those again who consider that the teaching hitherto given out in various books concerning initiation, is erroneous. Initiation has been made out to be fairly easy of attainment, and to call for no such rectitude of character as might have been anticipated. The following chapters may serve to show that the criticism is not un-merited. Initiation is profoundly difficult of attainment, and calls for a strenuous discipline of the entire lower nature, and a life of self-effacing and self-abnegating de-votion. At the same time, it must be remembered that the earlier teaching is right in essence, though belittled in in-terpretation.

Again, there are some who are interested, yet who feel the possibilities involved are too far advanced for them, and that they need not occupy themselves with them at this stage of their evolution. This book seeks to make it apparent that here and now the average man may begin to build that character and to lay those foundations of knowledge which are necessary before even the Path of Discipleship can be trodden. Due preparation may now be made, and men and women everywhere may—if they choose—fit themselves for the condition of discipleship and tread the Probationary Path.

Hundreds in the East and in the West are pressing on-wards towards this goal. and in the unity of the one ideal, in their common aspiration and endeavour, they will meet before the one Portal. They will then recognise them-selves as brothers, severed by tongue and apparent diversity of belief, but fundamentally holding to the same one truth and serving the same God.

Alice A. Bailey.

New York 1922.

EXTRACT FROM A STATEMENT BY THE TIBETAN

Published August 1934

Suffice it to say, that I am a Tibetan disciple of a certain degree, and this tells you but little, for all are disciples from the humblest aspirant up to, and beyond, the Christ Himself. I live in a physical body like other men, on the borders of Tibet, and at times (from the exoteric standpoint) preside over a large group of Tibetan lamas, when my other duties permit. It is this fact that has caused it to be reported that I am an abbot of this particular lamasery. Those associated with me in the work of the Hierarchy (and all true disciples are associated in this work) know me by still another name and office. A.A.B. knows who I am and recognises me by two of my names.

I am a brother of yours, who has travelled a little longer upon the Path than has the average student, and has therefore incurred greater responsibilities. I am one who has wrestled and fought his way into a greater measure of light than has the aspirant who will read this article, and I must therefore act as a transmitter of the light, no matter what the cost. I am not an old man, as age counts among the teachers, yet I am not young or inexperienced. My work is to teach and spread the knowledge of the Ageless Wisdom wherever I can find a response, and I have been doing this for many years. I seek also to help the Master M. and the Master K.H. whenever opportunity offers, for I have been long connected with Them and with Their work. In all the above, I have told you much; yet at the same time I have told you nothing which would lead you to offer me that blind obedience and the foolish devotion which the emotional aspirant offers to the Guru and Master whom he is as yet unable to contact. Nor will he make that desired contact until he has transmuted emotional devotion into unselfish service to humanity,—not to the Master.

The books that I have written are sent out with no claim for their acceptance. They may, or may not, be correct, true and useful. It is for you to ascertain their truth by right practice and by the exercise of the intuition. Neither I nor A.A.B. is the least interested in having them acclaimed as inspired writings, or in having anyone speak of them (with bated breath) as being the work of one of the Masters. If they present truth in such a way that it follows sequentially upon that already offered in the world teachings, if the information given raises the aspiration and the will-to-serve from the plane of the emotions to that of the mind (the plane whereon the Masters *can* be found) then they will have served their purpose. If the teaching conveyed calls forth a response from the illumined mind of the worker in the world, and brings a flashing forth of his intuition, then let that teaching be accepted. But not otherwise. If the statements meet with eventual corroboration, or are deemed true under the test of the Law of Correspondences, then that is well and good. But should this not be so, let not the student accept what is said.

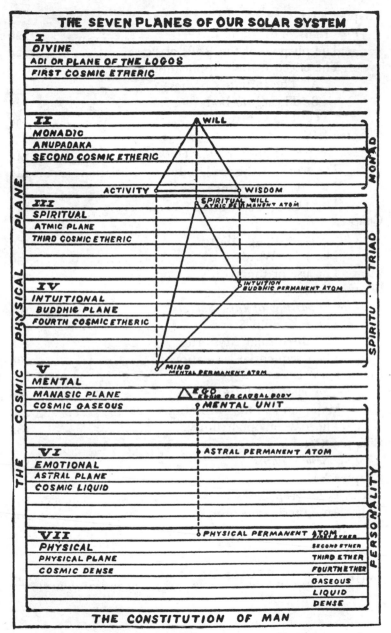

THE CONSTITUTION OF MAN

xiv

TABLE OF CONTENTS

THE CONSTITUTION OF MAN

The constitution of man, as considered in the following pages, is basically threefold, as follows:—

I. *The Monad, or pure Spirit, the Father in Heaven.*

This aspect reflects the three aspects of the Godhead:

    1. Will or Power . . . . The Father.

    2. Love-wisdom . . . . The Son.

    3. Active Intelligence . . . . The Holy Spirit.

and is only contacted at the final initiations, when man is nearing the end of his journey and is perfected. The Monad reflects itself again in

II. *The Ego, Higher Self, or Individuality.*

This aspect is potentially

    1. Spiritual Will . . . . Atma.

    2. Intuition . . . . Buddhi,
           Love-wisdom, the Christ principle.

    3. Higher or abstract Mind . . . . Higher Manas.

The Ego begins to make its power felt in advanced men, and increasingly on the Probationary Path until by the third initiation the control of the lower self by the higher is perfected, and the highest aspect begins to make its energy felt.

The Ego reflects itself in

III. *The Personality, or lower self, physical plane man.*

This aspect is also threefold:—

    1. A mental body . . . . lower manas.

    2. An emotional body . . . . astral body.

    3. A physical body . . . . the dense physical
           and the etheric body.

The aim of evolution is therefore to bring man to the realisation of the Egoic aspect and to bring the lower nature under its control.

INITIATION, HUMAN AND SOLAR

CHAPTER I

INTRODUCTORY REMARKS

Before entering upon the subject matter of the following articles on Initiation, on the Paths that open before
the perfected man, and on the Occult Hierarchy, certain
statements may be made which seem essential for the
judicious study and comprehension of the ideas submitted.

It is to be recognised that throughout this volume facts
are alleged and definite statements made which are not
susceptible of immediate proof by the reader. Lest it be
inferred that the writer arrogates to herself any credit or
personal authority for the knowledge implied she emphati-
cally disavows all such claims or representations. She cannot do otherwise than present these statements as matters
of fact. Nevertheless, she would urge those who find somewhat of merit in these pages that they be not estranged
by any appearance of dogmatism in the presentation. Nor
should the inadequacy of the personality of the writer act
as a deterrent to the open-minded consideration of the
message to which her name happens to be appended. In
spiritual issues, names, personalities, and the voice of exter-

nal authority, hold small place. That alone is a safe guide which holds its warranty from inner recognition and inner direction. It is not, therefore, material whether the reader receive the message of these pages as a spiritual appeal in an idealistic setting, a presentation of alleged facts, or a theory evolved by one student and presented for the consideration of fellow students. To each it is offered for whatever of inner response it may evoke, for whatever of inspiration and of light it may bring.

In these days of the shattering of the old form and the building of the new, adaptability is needed. We must avert the danger of crystallisation through pliability and expansion. The "old order changeth," but primarily it is a change of dimension and of aspect, and not of material or of foundation. The fundamentals have always been true. To each generation is given the part of conserving the essential features of the old and beloved form, but also of wisely expanding and enriching it. Each cycle must add the gain of further research and scientific endeavour, and subtract that which is worn out and of no value. Each age must build in the product and triumphs of its period, and abstract the accretions of the past that would dim and blur the outline. Above all, to each generation is given the joy of demonstrating the strength of the old foundations, and the opportunity to build upon these foundations a structure that will meet the needs of the inner evolving life.

The ideas that are elaborated here find their corroboration in certain facts that are stated in the occult literature now extant. These facts are three in number, and are as follows:—

(a) In the creation of the sun and the seven sacred planets composing our solar system, our Logos employed matter that was already impregnated with particular qualities. Mrs. Besant in her book, 'Avataras," (which some of us think the most valuable of all her writings, because one of the most suggestive), makes the statement that "our solar system is builded out of matter already existing, out of matter already gifted with certain properties . . . " (page 48). This matter, therefore, we deduce, held latent certain faculties that were forced to demonstrate in a peculiar way, under the law of Cause and Effect, as does all else in the universe.

(b) All manifestation is of a septenary nature, and the Central Light which we call Deity, the one Ray of Divinity, manifests first as a Triplicity, and then as a Septenary. The One God shines forth as God the Father, God the Son, and God the Holy Spirit, and these three are again reflected through the Seven Spirits before the Throne, or the seven Planetary Logoi. The students of occultism of non-Christian origin may call these Beings the One Ray, demonstrating through the three major Rays and the four minor, making a divine Septenary. The Synthetic Ray which blends them all is the great Love-Wisdom Ray, for verily and indeed "God is Love." This Ray is the indigo Ray, and is the blending Ray. It is the one which will, at the end of the greater cycle, absorb the others in the achievement of synthetic perfection. It is the manifestation of the second aspect of Logoic life. It is this aspect, that of the Form-Builder, that makes this solar system of ours the most concrete of the three major systems. The Love or Wisdom aspect demonstrates through the building of the form, for "God is Love," and in that God of Love we "live and move and have our being," and will to the end of aeonian manifestation.

(c) The seven planes of Divine Manifestation, or the seven major planes of our system, are but the seven sub-planes of the lowest cosmic plane. The seven Rays of which we hear so much, and which hold so much of interest and of mystery, are likewise but the seven sub-rays of one cosmic Ray. The twelve creative Hierarchies are themselves but subsidiary branches of one cosmic Hierarchy. They form but one chord in the cosmic symphony. When that seven-fold cosmic chord, of which we form so humble a part, reverberates in synthetic perfection, then, and only then, will come comprehension of the words in the Book of Job: "The morning stars sang together." Dissonance yet sounds forth, and discord arises from many systems, but in the progression of the aeons an ordered harmony will eventuate, and the day will dawn when (if we dare speak of eternities in the terms of time) the sound of the perfected universe will resound to the uttermost bounds of the furthest constellation. Then will be known the mystery of "the marriage song of the heavens."

The reader is also asked to remember and weigh certain ideas prior to taking up the study of Initiation. Due to the extreme complexity of the matter it is an utter impos-sibility for us to do more than get a general idea of the scheme; hence the futility of dogmatism. We can do no more than sense a fraction of some wonderful whole, utterly beyond the reach of our consciousness,—a whole that the highest Angel or Perfected Being is but beginning to realise. When we recognise the fact that the average man is as yet fully conscious only on the physical plane, nearly con-scious on the emotional plane, and only developing the consciousness of the mental plane, it is obvious that his comprehension of cosmic data can be but rudimentary. When we recognise the further fact, that to be *conscious* on a plane and to *have control* on that plane are two very different conditions, it becomes apparent how remote is the possibility of our approximating more than the general trend of the cosmic scheme.

We must recognise also that danger lies in dogma and in the hide-bound facts of textbooks, and that safety lies in flexibility, and in a shifting angle of vision. A fact, for instance, looked at from the standpoint of humanity (using the word "fact" in the scientific sense as that which has been demonstrated past all doubt and question) may not be a fact from the standpoint of a Master. To Him it may be but part of a greater fact, only a fraction of the whole. Since His vision is fourth and fifth dimensional, His realisation of the place of time in eternity must be more accurate than ours. He sees things from above downwards, and as one to whom time is not.

An inexplicable principle of mutation exists in the Mind of the Logos, or the Deity of our solar system, and governs all His actions. We see but the ever changing forms, and catch glimpses of the steadily evolving life within those forms, but as yet have no clue to the principle which works through the shifting kaleidoscope of solar systems, rays, hierarchies, planets, planes, schemes, rounds, races, and sub-races. They interweave, interlock, and interpenetrate each other, and utter bewilderment is ours as the wonderful pattern they form unfolds before us. We know that somewhere in that scheme we, the human hierarchy, have our place. All, therefore, that we can do is to seize upon any data that seems to affect our own welfare, and concerns our own evolution, and from the study of the human being in the three worlds seek to understand somewhat the macrocosm. We know not how the one can become the three, the three become the seven, and so proceed to inconceivable differentiation. To human vision this interweaving of the system forms an unimaginable complexity, the key to which seems not to be forthcoming. Seen from the angle of a Master we know that all proceeds in ordered sequence. Seen from the angle of divine vision the whole will move in harmonious unison, producing a form geometrically accurate. Browning had hold of a part of this truth when he wrote:

"All's change, but permanence as well"........and continued:

"Truth inside, and outside, truth also; and between each, falsehood that is change, as truth is permanence."

"Truth successively takes shape, one grade above its last presentment......"

We must remember also that beyond a certain point it is not safe nor wise to carry the communication of the facts of the solar system. Much must remain esoteric and veiled. The risks of too much knowledge are far greater than the menace of too little. With knowledge comes responsibility and power,—two things for which the race is not yet ready. Therefore, all we can do is to study and correlate with what wisdom and discretion may be ours, using the knowledge that may come for the good of those we seek to help, and recognising that in the wise use of knowledge comes increased capacity to receive the hidden wisdom. Coupled also with the wise adaptation of knowledge to the surrounding need must grow the capacity for discreet reservation, and the use of the discriminating faculty. When we can wisely use, discreetly withhold, and soundly discriminate, we give the surest guarantee to the watching Teachers of the race that we are ready for a fresh revelation.

We must resign ourselves to the fact that the only way in which we can find the clue to the mystery of the rays, systems, and hierarchies, lies in the study of the law of correspondences or analogy. It is the one thread by which we can find our way through the labyrinth, and the one ray of light that shines through the darkness of the surrounding ignorance. H. P. Blavatsky, in "The Secret Doctrine," has told us so, but as yet very little has been done by students to avail themselves of that clue. In the study of this Law we need to remember that the correspondence lies in its essence, and not in the exoteric working out of detail as we think we see it from our present standpoint. The factor of time leads us astray for one thing; we err when we attempt to fix stated times or limits; all in evolution progresses through merging, with a constant process of overlapping and mingling. Only broad generalities and a recognition of fundamental points of analogy are possible to the average student. The moment he attempts to reduce to chart form and to tabulate *in detail,* he enters realms where he is bound to err, and staggers through a fog that will ultimately overwhelm him.

Nevertheless, in the scientific study of this law of analogy will come a gradual growth of knowledge, and in the slow accumulation of facts will gradually be built up an ever-expanding form, that will embody much of the truth. The student will then awake to the realization that after all the study and toil he has at least a wide general conception of the Logoic thoughtform into which he can fit the details as he acquires them through many incarnations. This brings us to the last point to be considered before entering upon the subject proper, which is:

That the development of the human being is but the passing from one state of consciousness to another. It is a succession of expansions, a growth of that faculty of *awareness* that constitutes the predominant characteristic of the indwelling Thinker. It is the progressing from consciousness polarised in the personality, lower self, or body, to that polarised in the higher self, ego, or soul, thence to a polarisation in the Monad, or Spirit, till the consciousness eventually is Divine. As the human being develops, the faculty of awareness extends first of all beyond the circumscribing walls that confine it within the lower kingdoms of nature (the mineral, vegetable and animal) to the three worlds of the evolving personality, to the planet whereon he plays his part, to the system wherein that planet revolves, until it finally escapes from the solar system itself and becomes universal.

CHAPTER II

INITIATION DEFINED

The question anent initiation is one that is coming more and more before the public. Before many centuries pass the old mysteries will be restored, and an inner body will exist in the Church—the Church of the period, of which the nucleus is already forming—wherein the first initiation will become exoteric, in this sense only, that the taking of the first initiation will, before so very long, be the most sacred ceremony of the Church, performed exoterically as one of the mysteries given at stated periods, attended by those concerned. It will also hold a similar place in the ritual of the Masons. At this ceremony those ready for the first initiation will be publicly admitted to the Lodge by one of its members, authorised to do so by the great Hierophant Himself.

Four words defined.

When we speak of Initiation, of wisdom, of knowledge, or of the probationary Path, what do we mean? We use the words so glibly, without due consideration of the meaning involved. Take, for instance, the word first mentioned. Many are the definitions, and many are the explanations to be found as to its scope, the preparatory steps, the work to be done between initiations, and its result and effects. One thing before all else is apparent to the most superficial student, and that is, that the magnitude of the subject is such that in order to deal with it adequately one should be able to write from the viewpoint of an initiate; when this is not the case, anything that is said may be reasonable, logical, interesting, or suggestive, but not conclusive.

The word *Initiation* comes from two Latin words, *in,* into; and *ire,* to go; therefore, *the making of a beginning,* or the entrance into something. It posits, in its widest sense, in the case we are studying, an entrance into the spiritual life, or into a fresh stage in that life. It is the first step, and the succeeding steps, upon the Path of Holiness. Literally, therefore, a man who has taken the first initiation is one who has taken the first step into the spiritual kingdom, having passed out of the definitely human kingdom into the superhuman. Just as he passed out of the animal kingdom into the human at individualisation, so he has entered upon the life of the spirit, and for the first time has the right to be called a "spiritual man" in the technical significance of the word. He is entering upon the fifth or final stage in our present fivefold evolution. Having groped his way through the Hall of Ignorance during many ages, and having gone to school in the Hall of Learning, he is now entering into the university, or the Hall of Wisdom. When he has passed through that school he will graduate with his degree as a Master of Compassion.

It might be of benefit to us also if we studied first the difference or the connection between *Knowledge, Understanding,* and *Wisdom.* Though in ordinary parlance they are frequently interchanged, as used technically they are dissimilar.

Knowledge is the product of the Hall of Learning. It might be termed the sumtotal of human discovery and experience, that which can be recognised by the five senses, and be correlated, diagnosed, and defined by the use of the human intellect. It is that about which we feel mental certitude, or that which we can ascertain by the use of experiment. It is the compendium of the arts and sciences. It concerns all that deals with the building and developing of the form side of things. Therefore it concerns the material side of evolution, matter in the solar systems, in the planet, in the three worlds of human evolution, and in the bodies of men.

Wisdom is the product of the Hall of Wisdom. It has to do with the development of the life within the form, with the progress of the spirit through those ever-changing vehicles, and with the expansions of consciousness that succeed each other from life to life. It deals with the life side of evolution. Since it deals with the essence of things and not with the things themselves, it is the intuitive apprehension of truth apart from the reasoning faculty, and the innate perception that can distinguish between the false and the true, between the real and the unreal. It is more than that, for it is also the growing capacity of the Thinker to enter increasingly into the mind of the Logos, to realise the true inwardness of the great pageant of the universe, to vision the objective, and to harmonise more and more with the higher measure. For our present purpose (which is to study somewhat the Path of Holiness and its various stages) it may be described as the realisation of the "Kingdom of God within," and the apprehension of the "Kingdom of God without" in the solar system. Perhaps it might be expressed as the gradual blending of the paths of the mystic and the occultist,—the rearing of the temple of wisdom upon the foundation of knowledge.

Wisdom is the science of the spirit, just as knowledge is the science of matter. Knowledge is separative and objective, whilst wisdom is synthetic and subjective. Knowledge divides; wisdom unites. Knowledge differentiates whilst wisdom blends. What, then, is meant by the under-standing?

The understanding may be defined as the faculty of the Thinker in Time to appropriate knowledge as the foundation for wisdom, that which enables him to adapt the things of form to the life of the spirit, and to take the flashes of inspiration that come to him from the Hall of Wisdom and link them to the facts of the Hall of Learning. Perhaps the whole idea might be expressed in this way:

Wisdom concerns the one Self, knowledge deals with the not-self, whilst the understanding is the point of view of the Ego, or Thinker, or his relation between them.

In the Hall of Ignorance the form controls, and the material side of things has the predominance. Man is there polarised in the personality or lower self. In the Hall of Learning the higher self, or Ego, strives to dominate that form until gradually a point of equilibrium is reached where the man is controlled entirely by neither. Later the Ego controls more and more, until in the Hall of Wisdom it dominates in the three lower worlds, and in increasing degree the inherent divinity assumes the mastery.

Aspects of initiation.

Initiation, or the process of undergoing an expansion of consciousness, is part of the normal process of evolution-ary development, viewed on a large scale, and not from the standpoint of the individual. When viewed from the indi-vidual standpoint it has come to be narrowed down to the moment wherein the evolving unit definitely apprehends that (by dint of his own effort, aided by the advice and suggestions of the watching Teachers of the race) he has reached a point wherein a certain range of knowledge of a subjective nature, from the physical plane point of view, is his. It is in the nature of that experience wherein a pupil in a school realises suddenly that he has mastered a lesson, and that the rationale of a subject, and the method of procedure, are his to use intelligently. These moments of intelligent apprehension follow the evolving Monad throughout his long pilgrimage. What has been misinterpreted somewhat at this stage of comprehension is the fact that at various periods the emphasis is laid on different grades of expansion, and always the Hierarchy endeavours to bring the race to the point where its units will have some idea of the next step to be taken.

Each initiation marks the passing of the pupil in the Hall of Wisdom into a higher class, marks the clearer shining forth of the inner fire and the transition from one point of polarisation to another, entails the realisation of an increasing unity with all that lives and the essential oneness of the self with all selves. It results in a horizon that continuously enlarges until it includes the sphere of creation; it is a growing capacity to see and hear on all the planes. It is an increased consciousness of God's plans for the world, and an increased ability to enter into those plans and to further them. It is the effort in the abstract mind to pass an examination. It is the honour class in the Master's school, and is within the attainment of those souls whose karma permits and whose efforts suffice to fulfil the aim.

Initiation leads to the mount whence vision can be had, a vision of the eternal Now, wherein past, present, and future exist as one; a vision of the pageant of the races with the golden thread of pedigree carried through the many types; a vision of the golden sphere that holds in unison all the many evolutions of our system, deva, human, animal, vegetable, mineral, and elemental, and through which the pulsating life can be clearly seen beating in regular rhythm;

a vision of the Logoic thoughtform on the archetypal plane, a vision that grows from initiation to initiation until it embraces all the solar system.

Initiation leads to the stream that, once entered, sweeps a man onward until it carries him to the feet of the Lord of the World, to the feet of his Father in Heaven, to the feet of the three-fold Logos.

Initiation leads to the cave within whose circumscribing walls the pairs of opposites are known, and the secret of good and evil is revealed. It leads to the Cross and to that utter sacrifice which must transpire before perfect liberation is attained, and the initiate stands free of all earth's fetters, held by naught in the three worlds. It leads through the Hall of Wisdom, and puts into a man's hands the key to all information, systemic and cosmic, in graduated sequence. It reveals the hidden mystery that lies at the heart of the solar system. It leads from one state of consciousness to another. As each state is entered the horizon enlarges, the vista extends, and the comprehension includes more and more, until the expansion reaches a point where the self embraces all selves, including all that is "moving and unmoving," as phrased by an ancient Scripture.

Initiation involves ceremony. It is this aspect that has been emphasised in the minds of men, perhaps a little to the exclusion of the true significance. Primarily it involves the capacity to see, hear, and comprehend, and to synthesise and correlate knowledge. It does not necessarily involve the development of the psychic faculties, but it does entail the inner comprehension that sees the value underlying the form, and recognises the purpose of pervading circumstances. It is the capacity that senses the lesson to be learnt from any given occurrence and event, and that by means of these comprehensions and recognitions effects an hourly, weekly, yearly growth and expansion. This process of gradual expansion—the result of the definite effort and strenuous right thinking and living of the aspirant himself and not of some occult teacher performing an occult rite—leads to what one might term a *crisis*.

At this crisis, which necessitates the aid of a Master, a definite act of initiation is performed, which (acting on a particular centre) produces a result on some one body. It keys the atoms to a certain pitch, and enables a new rate of rhythm to be attained.

This ceremony of initiation marks a point of attainment. It does not bring about attainment, as is so often the misconception. It simply marks the recognition by the watching Teachers of the race of a definite point in evolution reached by the pupil, and gives two things:—

1. An expansion of consciousness that admits the personality into the wisdom attained by the Ego, and in the higher initiations into the consciousness of the Monad.

2. A brief period of enlightenment wherein the initiate sees that portion of the Path that lies ahead to be trodden, and wherein he shares consciously in the great plan of evolution.

After initiation, the work to be done consists largely in making that expansion of consciousness part of the equipment for the practical use of the personality, and in mastering that portion of the path that has yet to be traversed.

The place and effect of initiation.

The ceremony of initiation takes place on the three higher sub-planes of the mental plane, and on the three higher planes, according to the initiation. The five-pointed star, at the initiations on the mental plane, flashes out above the head of the initiate. This concerns the first initiations which are undergone in the causal vehicle. It has been said that the first two initiations take place upon the astral plane, but this is incorrect, and the statement has given rise to a misunderstanding. They are felt profoundly in connection with the astral and physical bodies and the lower mental, and affect their control. The chief effect being felt in those bodies the initiate may interpret them as having taken place on the planes concerned, as the vividness of the effect and the stimulation of the first two initiations work out largely in the astral body. But it must ever be remembered that the major initiations are taken in the causal body or—dissociated from that body—on the buddhic plane or atmic plane. At the final two initiations which set a man free from the three worlds, and enable him to function in the body of vitality of the Logos and wield that force, the initiate becomes the five-pointed star and it descends upon him, merges in him, and he is seen at its very centre. This descent is brought about by the action of the Initiator, wielding the Rod of Power, and puts a man in touch with the centre in the Body of the Planetary Logos of which he is a part, and this consciously. The two initiations called the sixth and seventh take place on the buddhic and atmic planes; the five-pointed star "blazes forth from within Itself," as the esoteric phrase has it, and becomes the seven-pointed star; it descends upon the man and he enters within the flame.

Again, the four initiations, prior to that of the adept, mark respectively the attainment of certain proportions of atomic matter in the bodies—for instance, at the first initiation one-fourth atomic matter, at the second one-half atomic matter, at the third three-quarters atomic matter, and so on to the completion. Since buddhi is the unifying principle (or the welder of all), at the fifth initiation the adept lets the lower vehicles go, and stands in his buddhic sheath. He creates thence his body of manifestation.

Each initiation gives more control on the rays, if one may so express it, although this does not adequately convey the idea. Words so often mislead. At the fifth initiation, when the adept stands Master in the three worlds, He controls more or less (according to His line of development) the five rays that are specially manifesting at the time He takes the initiation. At the sixth initiation, if He takes the higher degree, He gains power on another ray, and at the seventh initiation He wields power on all the rays. The sixth initiation marks the point of attainment of the Christ, and brings the synthetic ray of the system under His control. We need to remember that initiation gives the initiate *power on the rays,* and not *power over the rays,* for this marks a very definite difference. Every initiate has, of course, for his primary or spiritual ray one of the three major rays, and the ray of his Monad is the one on which he at length gains power. The love ray, or the synthetic ray of the system, is the final one achieved.

Those who pass away from the earth after the fifth initiation, or those who do not become Masters in physical incarnation, take their subsequent initiations elsewhere in the system. All are in the Logoic Consciousness. One great fact to be borne in mind is, that the initiations of the planet or of the solar system are but the preparatory initiations of admission into the greater Lodge on Sirius. We have the symbolism held for us fairly well in Masonry, and in combining the Masonic method with what we are told of the steps on the Path of Holiness we get an approximate picture. Let us enlarge somewhat:—

The first four initiations of the solar system correspond to the four "initiations of the Threshold," prior to the first cosmic initiation. The fifth initiation corresponds to the first cosmic initiation, that of "entered apprentice" in Masonry; and makes a Master an "entered apprentice" of the Lodge on Sirius. The sixth initiation is analogous to the second degree in Masonry, whilst the seventh initiation makes the Adept a Master Mason of the Brotherhood on Sirius.

A Master, therefore, is one who has taken the seventh planetary initiation, the fifth solar initiation, and the first Sirian or cosmic initiation.

At-one-ment, the result of initiation.

A point that we need to grasp is that each successive initiation brings about a more complete unification of the personality and the Ego, and on higher levels still, with the Monad. The whole evolution of the human spirit is a progressive at-one-ment. In the at-one-ment between the Ego and the personality lies hid the mystery of the Christian doctrine of the Atonement. One unification takes place at the moment of individualisation, when man becomes a conscious rational entity, in contradistinction to the animals. As evolution proceeds successive at-one-ments occur.

At-one-ment on all levels—emotional, intuitional, spiritual and Divine—consists in conscious, continuous functioning. In all cases it is preceded by a burning, through the medium of the inner fire, and by the destruction, through sacrifice, of all that separates. The approach to unity is through destruction of the lower, and of all that forms a barrier. Take, in illustration, the web that separates the etheric body and the emotional. When that web has been burned away by the inner fire the communication between the bodies of the personality becomes continuous and complete, and the three lower vehicles function as one. You have a somewhat analogous situation on the higher levels, though the parallel cannot be pushed to detail. The intuition corresponds to the emotional, and the four higher levels of the mental plane to the etheric. In the destruction of the causal body at the time of the fourth initiation (called symbolically "the Crucifixion") you have a process analogous to the burning of the web that leads to the unification of the bodies of the personality. The disintegration that is a part of the arhat initiation leads to unity between the Ego and the Monad, expressing itself in the Triad. It is the perfect at-one-ment.

The whole process is therefore for the purpose of making man consciously one:—

First: With himself, and those in incarnation with him.

Second: With his higher Self, and thus with all selves.

Third: With his Spirit, or "Father in Heaven," and thus with all Monads.

Fourth: With the Logos, the Three in One and the One in Three.

Man becomes a conscious human being through the instrumentality of the Lords of the Flame, through Their enduring sacrifice.

Man becomes a conscious Ego, with the consciousness of the higher Self, at the third initiation, through the instrumentality of the Masters and of the Christ, and through Their sacrifice in taking physical incarnation for the helping of the world.

Man unites with the Monad at the fifth initiation, through the instrumentality of the Lord of the World, the Solitary Watcher, the Great Sacrifice.

Man becomes one with the Logos through the instrumentality of *One about Whom naught may be said*.

CHAPTER III

THE WORK OF THE HIERARCHY

Though the subject of the occult Hierarchy of the planet is of such a profoundly momentous interest to the average man, yet its real significance will never be understood until men realise three things in connection with it. First, that the entire Hierarchy of spiritual beings represents a synthesis of forces or of energies, which forces or energies are consciously manipulated for the furtherance of planetary evolution. This will become more apparent as we proceed. Secondly, that these forces, demonstrating in our planetary scheme through those great Personalities Who compose the Hierarchy, link it and all that it contains with the greater Hierarchy which we call Solar. Our Hierarchy is a miniature replica of the greater synthesis of those selfconscious Entities who manipulate, control, and demonstrate through the sun and the seven sacred planets, as well as the other planets, greater and smaller, of which our solar system is composed. Thirdly, that this Hierarchy of forces has four pre-eminent lines of work:—

To develop selfconsciousness in all beings.

The Hierarchy seeks to provide fit conditions for the development of selfconsciousness in all beings. This it produces primarily in man through its initial work of blending the higher three aspects of spirit with the lower four; through the example it sets of service, sacrifice, and renunciation, and through the constant streams of light (occultly understood) which emanate from it. The Hierarchy might be considered as the aggregate on our planet of the forces of the fifth kingdom in nature. This kingdom is entered through the full development and control of the fifth principle of mind, and its transmutation into wisdom, which is literally the intelligence applied to all states through the full conscious utilisation of the faculty of discriminative love.

To develop consciousness in the three lower kingdoms.

As is well known, the five kingdoms of nature on the evolutionary arc might be defined as follows:—the mineral kingdom, the vegetable kingdom, the animal kingdom, the human kingdom, and the spiritual kingdom. All these kingdoms embody some type of consciousness, and it is the work of the Hierarchy to develop these types to perfection through the adjustment of karma, through the agency of force, and through the providing of right conditions. Some idea of the work may be gained if we briefly summarize the different aspects of consciousness to be developed in the various kingdoms.

In the *mineral kingdom* the work of the Hierarchy is directed toward the development of the discriminative and selective activity. One characteristic of all matter is activity of some kind, and the moment that activity is directed towards the building of forms, even of the most elemental kind, the faculty of discrimination will demonstrate. This is recognised by scientists everywhere, and in this recognition they are approximating the findings of the Divine Wisdom.

In the *vegetable kingdom,* to this faculty of discrimination is added that of response to sensation, and the rudimentary condition of the second aspect of divinity is to be seen, just as in the mineral kingdom a similar rudimentary reflection of the third aspect of activity is making itself felt.

In the *animal kingdom* this rudimentary activity and feeling are increased, and symptoms (if it might be so inadequately expressed) are to be found of the first aspect, or embryonic will and purpose; we may call it hereditary instinct, but it works out in fact as purpose in nature.

It has been wisely stated by H. P. Blavatsky that man is the macrocosm for the three lower kingdoms, for in him these three lines of development are synthesised and come to their full fruition. He is verily and indeed intelligence, actively and wonderfully manifested; He is incipient love and wisdom, even though as yet they may be but the goal of his endeavour; and he has that embryonic, dynamic, initiating will which will come to a fuller development after he has entered into the fifth kingdom.

In the fifth kingdom, the consciousness to be developed is that of the group, and this shows itself in the full flowering of the love-wisdom faculty. Man but repeats on a higher turn of the spiral, the work of the three lower kingdoms, for in the human kingdom he shows forth the third aspect of active intelligence. In the fifth kingdom, which is entered at the first initiation, and which covers all the period of time wherein a man takes the first five initiations, and that wherein he works as a Master, as part of the Hierarchy, the love-wisdom, or second aspect, comes to its consummation. At the sixth and seventh initiations the first, or will, aspect shines forth, and from being a Master of Compassion and a Lord of Love the adept becomes something more. He enters into a still higher consciousness than that of the group, and becomes God-conscious. The great will or purpose of the Logos becomes his.

The fostering of the various attributes of divinity, the tending of the seed of selfconsciousness in all beings, is the work of those Entities who have achieved, Who have entered into the fifth kingdom and Who have there made Their great decision, and that inconceivable renunciation which leads Them to stay within the planetary scheme, and thus co-operate with the plans of the Planetary Logos on the physical plane.

To transmit the will of the Planetary Logos,

They act as the transmitter to men and devas or angels, of the will of the Planetary Logos, and through Him of the Solar Logos. Each planetary scheme, ours amongst the others, is a centre in the body Logoic, and is expressing some form of energy or force. Each centre expresses its particular type of force, demonstrated in a triple manner, producing thus universally the three aspects in manifestation. One of the great realisations which come to those who enter into the fifth kingdom is that of the particular type of force which our own Planetary Logos embodies. The wise student will ponder on this statement, for it holds the clue to much that may be seen in the world today. The secret of synthesis has been lost, and only when men again get back the knowledge which was theirs in earlier cycles (having been mercifully withdrawn in Atlantean days) of the type of energy which our scheme should be demonstrating, will the world problems adjust themselves, and the world rhythm be stabilised. This cannot be as yet, for this knowledge is of a dangerous kind, and at present the race as a whole is not group conscious, and therefore cannot be trusted to work, think, plan, and act for the group. Man is as yet too selfish, but there is no cause for discouragement in this fact; group consciousness is already somewhat more than a vision, whilst brotherhood, and the recognition of its obligations, is beginning to permeate the consciousness of men everywhere. This is the work of the Hierarchy of Light,—to demonstrate to men the true meaning of brotherhood, and to foster in them response to that ideal which is latent in one and all.

To set an example to humanity.

The fourth thing that men need to know and to realise as a basic fact is that this Hierarchy is composed of those Who have triumphed over matter, and Who have achieved the goal by the very self-same steps that individuals tread today. These spiritual personalities, these adepts and Masters, have wrestled and fought for victory and mastery upon the physical plane, and struggled with the miasmas, the fogs, the dangers, the troubles, the sorrows and pains of everyday living. They have trodden every step of the path of suffering, have undergone every experience, have surmounted every difficulty, and have won out. These Elder Brothers of the race have one and all undergone the crucifixion of the personal self, and know that utter renunciation of all which is the lot of every aspirant at this time. There is no phase of agony, no rending sacrifice, no Via Dolorosa that They have not in Their time trodden, and herein lies Their right to serve, and the strength of the method of Their appeal. Knowing the quintessence of pain, knowing the depth of sin and of suffering, Their methods can be exquisitely measured to the individual need; yet at the same time Their realisation of the liberation to be achieved through pain, penalty, and suffering, and Their apprehension of the freedom that comes through the sacrifice of the form by the medium of the purificatory fires, suffices to give Them a firm hand, an ability to persist even when the form may seem to have undergone a sufficiency of suffering, and a love that triumphs over all setbacks, for it is founded on patience and experience. These Elder Brothers of humanity are characterised by a *love* which endures, and which acts ever for the good of the group; by a *knowledge* which has been gained through a millennia of lives, in which They have worked Their way from the bottom of life and of evolution well nigh to the top; by an *experience* which is based on time itself and a multiplicity of personality reactions and interactions; by a *courage* which is the result of that experience, and which, having itself been produced by ages of endeavour, failure, and renewed endeavour, and having in the long run led to triumph, can now be placed at the service of the race; by a *purpose* which is enlightened and intelligent, and which is co-operative, adjusting itself to the group and hierarchical plan and thus fitting in with the purpose of the Planetary Logos; and finally They are distinguished by a knowledge of the *power of sound.* This final fact is the basis of that aphorism which states that all true occultists are distinguished by the characteristics of knowledge, dynamic will, courage, and silence. "To know, to will, to dare, and to be silent." Knowing the plan so well, and having clear, illuminated vision, They can bend Their will unflinchingly and unswervingly to the great work of creation by the power of sound. This leads to Their silence where the average man would speak, and Their speaking where the average man is silent.

When men have grasped the four facts here enumerated, and they are established as acknowledged truths in the consciousness of the race, then may we look for a return of that cycle of peace and rest and righteousness which is foretold in all the Scriptures of the world. The Sun of Righteousness will then arise with healing in His wings, and the peace which passeth understanding will reign in the hearts of men.

In dealing with this matter of the work of the occult Hierarchy, in a book for the general public, much must be left unsaid. The average man is interested and his curiosity is aroused by reference to these Personalities, but men are not yet ready for more than the most general information. For those who, from curiosity, pass on to desire and seek to know the truth as it is, more will be forthcoming, when they themselves have done the necessary work and study. Investigation is desired, and the attitude of mind which it is hoped this book will arouse might be summed up in the following words:—These statements sound interesting and perchance they are true. The religions of all nations, the Christian included, give indications that seem to substantiate these ideas. Let us therefore accept these ideas as a working hypothesis as to the consummation of the evolutionary process in man and his work upon the attainment of perfection. Let us therefore seek for the truth as a fact in our own consciousness. Every religious faith holds out the promise that those who seek with earnestness shall find that which they are seeking; let us, therefore, seek. If by our search we find that all these statements are but visionary dreams, and profit not at all, leading us only into darkness, time will nevertheless not have been lost, for we shall have ascertained where not to look. If by our search, on the other hand, corroboration comes little by little, and the light shines ever more clearly, let us persist until that day dawns when the light which shineth in darkness will have illuminated the heart and brain, and the seeker will awaken to the realisation that the whole trend of evolution has been to bring him this expansion of consciousness and this illumination, and that the attainment of the initiatory process, and the entrance into the fifth kingdom is no wild chimera or phantasm, but an established fact in the consciousness. This each man must ascertain for himself. Those who know may state a fact to be thus and so, but the dictum of another person and the enunciation of a theory do not aid beyond giving to the seeker confirmatory indication. Each soul has to ascertain for himself, and must find out within himself, remembering ever that the kingdom of God is within, and that only those facts which are realised within the individual consciousness as truths are of any real value. In the meantime, that which many know, and have ascertained within themselves to be truths of an incontrovertible nature for them, may here be stated; to the intelligent reader will then arise the opportunity and the responsibility of ascertaining for himself their falsity or truth.

CHAPTER IV

THE FOUNDING OF THE HIERARCHY

Its appearance on the planet.

It is not sought, in this book, to deal with the steps which led to the founding of the Hierarchy on the planet, nor to consider the conditions preceding the advent of those great Beings. This can be studied in other occult books in the occident, and in the sacred Scriptures of the East. Suffice it for our purpose to say that in the middle of the Lemurian epoch, approximately eighteen million years ago, occurred a great event which signified, among other things, the following developments:—The Planetary Logos of our earth scheme, one of the Seven Spirits before the throne, took physical incarnation, and, under the form of Sanat Kumara, the Ancient of Days, and the Lord of the World, came down to this dense physical planet and has remained with us ever since. Owing to the extreme purity of His nature, and the fact that He is (from the human standpoint) relatively sinless, and hence incapable of response to aught on the dense physical plane, He was unable to take a dense physical body such as ours, and has to function in His etheric body. He is the greatest of all the Avatars, or Coming Ones, for He is a direct reflection of that great Entity who lives, and breathes, and functions through all the evolutions on this planet, holding all within His aura or magnetic sphere of influence. In Him we live and move and have our being, and none of us can pass beyond the radius of His aura. He is the Great Sacrifice, Who left the glory of the high places and for the sake of the evolving sons of men took upon Himself a physical form and was made in the likeness of man. He is the Silent Watcher, as far as our immediate humanity is concerned, although literally the Planetary Logos Himself, on the higher plane of consciousness whereon He functions, is the true Silent Watcher where the planetary scheme is concerned. Perhaps it might be stated thus:— That the Lord of the World, the One Initiator, holds the same place in connection with the Planetary Logos as the physical manifestation of a Master holds to that Master's Monad on the monadic plane. In both cases the intermediate state of consciousness has been superseded, that of the Ego or higher self, and that which we see and know is the *direct* self-created manifestation of pure spirit itself. Hence the sacrifice. It must here be borne in mind that in the case of Sanat Kumara there is a tremendous difference in degree, for His point in evolution is as far in advance of that of an adept as that adept's is in advance of animal man. This will be somewhat elaborated in the next section of our subject.

With the Ancient of Days came a group of other highly evolved Entities, who represent His own individual karmic group and those Beings who are the outcome of the triple nature of the Planetary Logos. If one might so express it They embody the forces emanating from the head, heart, and throat centres, and They came in with Sanat Kumara to form focal points of planetary force for the helping of the great plan for the self-conscious unfoldment of all life. Their places have gradually been filled by the sons of men as they qualify, though this includes very few, until lately, from our immediate earth humanity. Those who are now the inner group around the Lord of the World have been primarily recruited from the ranks of those who were initiates on the moon chain (the cycle of evolution preceding ours) or who have come in on certain streams of solar energy, astrologically determined, from other planetary schemes, yet those who have triumphed in our own humanity are rapidly increasing in number, and hold all the minor offices beneath the central esoteric group of Six, who, with the Lord of the World, form the heart of hierarchial effort.

The immediate effect.

The result of Their advent, millions of years ago, was stupendous, and its effects are still being felt. Those effects might be enumerated as follows:—The Planetary Logos on His own plane was enabled to take a more direct method in producing the results He desired for working out His plan. As is well known, the planetary scheme, with its dense globe and inner subtler globes, is to the Planetary Logos what the physical body and its subtler bodies are to man. Hence in illustration it might be said that the coming into incarnation of Sanat Kumara was analogous to the firm grip of self-conscious control that the Ego of a human being takes upon his vehicles when the necessary stage in evolution has been achieved. It has been said that in the head of every man are seven centres of force, which are linked to the other centres in the body, and through which the force of the Ego is spread and circulated, thus working out the plan. Sanat Kumara, with the six other Kumaras, holds a similar position. These central seven are as the seven head centres to the body corporate. They are the directing agents and the transmitters of the energy, force, purpose, and will of the Planetary Logos on His own plane. This planetary head centre works directly through the heart and throat centres, and thereby controls all the remaining centres. This is by way of illustration, and an attempt to show the relation of the Hierarchy to its planetary source, and also the close analogy between the method of functioning of a Planetary Logos and of man, the microcosm.

The third kingdom of nature, the animal kingdom, had reached a relatively high state of evolution, and animal man was in possession of the earth; he was a being with a powerful physical body, a co-ordinated astral body, or body of sensation and feeling, and a rudimentary germ of mind which might some day form a nucleus of a mental body. Left to himself for long aeons animal man would have eventually progressed out of the animal kingdom into the human, and would have become a self-conscious, functioning, rational entity, but how slow the process would have been may be evidenced by the study of the bushmen of South Africa, the Veddhas of Ceylon, and the hairy Ainus.

The decision of the Planetary Logos to take a physical vehicle produced an extraordinary stimulation in the evolutionary process, and by His incarnation, and the methods of force distribution He employed, He brought about in a brief cycle of time what would otherwise have been inconceivably slow. The germ of mind in animal man was stimulated. The fourfold lower man,

> a. The physical body in its dual capacity, etheric and dense,
> b. Vitality, life force, or prana,
> c. The astral or emotional body,
> d. The incipient germ of mind.

was co-ordinated and stimulated, and became a fit receptacle for the coming in of the self-conscious entities, those spiritual triads (the reflection of spiritual will, intuition, or wisdom, and higher mind) who had for long ages been waiting for just such a fitting. The fourth, or human kingdom, came thus into being, and the self-conscious, or rational unit, man, began his career.

Another result of the advent of the Hierarchy was a similar, though less recognised development in all the kingdoms of nature. In the mineral kingdom, for instance, certain of the minerals or elements received an added stimulation, and became radioactive, and a mysterious chemical change took place in the vegetable kingdom. This facilitated the bridging process between the vegetable and animal kingdoms, just as the radio-activity of minerals is the method of bridging the gulf between the mineral and vegetable kingdoms. In due course of time scientists will recognise that every kingdom in nature is linked and entered when the units of that kingdom become radioactive. But it is not necessary for us to digress along these lines. A hint suffices for those who have eyes to see, and the intuition to comprehend the meaning conveyed by terms which are handicapped by having a purely material connotation.

In Lemurian days, after the great descent of the spiritual Existences to the earth, the work They planned to do was systematised. Offices were apportioned, and the processes of evolution in all the departments of nature were brought under the conscious wise guidance of this initial Brotherhood. This Hierarchy of Brothers of Light still exists, and the work goes steadily on. They are all in physical existence, either in dense physical bodies, such as many of the Masters employ, or in etheric bodies, such as the more exalted helpers and the Lord of the World occupy. It is of value for men to remember that They are in physical existence, and to bear in mind that They exist upon this planet with us, controlling its destinies, guiding its affairs, and leading all its evolutions on to an ultimate perfection.

The central home of this Hierarchy is at Shamballa, a centre in the Gobi desert, called in the ancient books the "White Island." It exists in etheric matter, and when the race of men on earth have developed etheric vision its location will be recognised and its reality admitted. The development of this vision is rapidly coming to pass, as may be seen from the newspapers and the current literature of the day, but the location of Shamballa will be one of the latest etheric sacred spots to be revealed as it exists in the matter of the second ether. Several of the Masters in physical bodies dwell in the Himalaya mountains, in a secluded spot called Shigatse, far from the ways of men, but the greater number are scattered all over the world, dwelling in different places in the various nations, unrecognised and unknown, yet forming each in His own place a focal point for the energy of the Lord of the World, and proving to His environment a distributor of the love and wisdom of the Deity.

The opening of the Door of Initiation.

It is not possible to touch upon the history of the Hierarchy during the long ages of its work, beyond mentioning certain outstanding events of the past, and pointing out certain eventualities. For ages after its immediate founding, the work was slow and discouraging. Thousands of years came and went, and races of men appeared and disappeared from the earth before it was possible to delegate even the work done by initiates of the first degree to the evolving sons of men. But in the middle of the fourth root-race, the Atlantean, an event occurred which necessitated a change, or innovation in the Hierarchical method. Certain of its members were called away to higher work elsewhere in the solar system, and this brought in, through necessity, a number of highly evolved units of the human family. In order to enable others to take Their place, the lesser members of the Hierarchy were all moved up a step, leaving vacancies among the minor posts. Therefore three things were decided upon in the Council Chamber of the Lord of the World.

1. To close the door through which animal men passed into the human kingdom, permitting for a time no more Monads on the higher plane to appropriate bodies. This restricted the number of the fourth, or human kingdom, to its then limitation.

2. To open another door, and permit members of the human family who were willing to undergo the necessary discipline and to make the required stupendous effort, to enter the fifth or spiritual kingdom. In this way the ranks of the Hierarchy could be filled by the members of earth's humanity who qualified. This door is called the Portal of Initiation, and still remains open upon the same terms as laid down by the Lord of the World in Atlantean days. These terms will be stated in the last chapter of this book. The door between the human and animal kingdoms will again be opened during the next great cycle, or "round" as it is called in some books, but as this is several million years away from us at this time, we are not concerned with it.

3. It was also decided to make the line of demarcation between the two forces of matter and spirit clearly defined; the inherent duality of all manifestation was emphasised, with the aim in view of teaching men how to liberate themselves from the limitations of the fourth, or human kingdom, and thus pass on into the fifth, or spiritual. The problem of good or evil, light or darkness, right or wrong, was enunciated solely for the benefit of humanity, and to enable men to cast off the fetters which im-

prisoned spirit, and thus achieve spiritual freedom. This problem exists not in the kingdoms below man, nor for those who transcend the human. Man has to learn through experience and pain the fact of the duality of all existence. Having thus learnt, he chooses that which concerns the fully conscious spirit aspect of divinity, and learns to centre himself in that aspect. Having thus achieved liberation he finds indeed that all is one, that spirit and matter are a unity, naught existing save that which is to be found within the consciousness of the Planetary Logos, and—in wider circles—within the consciousness of the Solar Logos.

The Hierarchy thus took advantage of the discriminative faculty of mind, which is the distinctive quality of humanity, to enable him, through the balancing of the pairs of opposites, to reach his goal, and to find his way back to the source from whence he came.

This decision led to that great struggle which distinguished the Atlantean civilisation, and which culminated in the destruction called the flood, referred to in all the Scriptures of the world. The forces of light, and the forces of darkness, were arrayed against each other, and this for the helping of humanity. The struggle still persists, and the World War through which we have just passed was a recrudescence of it. On every side in that World War two groups were to be found, those who fought for an ideal as they saw it, for the highest that they knew, and those who fought for material and selfish advantage. In the struggle of these influential idealists or materialists many were swept in who fought blindly and ignorantly, being thus overwhelmed with racial karma and disaster.

These three decisions of the Hierarchy are having, and will have a profound effect upon humanity, but the result desired is being achieved, and a rapid hastening of the evolutionary process, and a profoundly important effect upon the mind aspect in man, can already be seen.

It might here be well to point out that, working as members of that Hierarchy are a great number of beings called angels by the Christian, and devas by the oriental. Many of them have passed through the human stage long ages ago, and work now in the ranks of the great evolution parallel to the human, and which is called the deva evolution. This evolution comprises among other factors, the builders of the objective planet and the forces which produce, through those builders, every form familiar and unfamiliar. The devas who co-operate with the Hierarchical effort, concern themselves, therefore, with the form aspect, whilst the other members of the Hierarchy are occupied with the development of consciousness within the form.

CHAPTER V

THE THREE DEPARTMENTS OF THE HIERARCHY

We have already dealt with the subject of the founding of the Hierarchy upon earth, and we saw how it came to be, touching likewise upon certain crises which have occurred, and which still affect events in the present time. In dealing with the work and aims of the personnel of the Hierarchy, it will not be possible to state what those aims have been, nor to consider in detail who the active personalities have been during the past millennia of years since the Hierarchy came into existence.

Many great Beings from planetary and solar sources, and once or twice from cosmic sources, have at times lent Their aid and dwelt briefly upon our planet. By the energy which flowed through Them, and by Their profound wisdom and experience, They stimulated earth's evolutions and brought the purposes of the Planetary Logos so much the nearer to completion. Then They passed on, and Their places were taken by those among the members of the Hierarchy Who were willing to undergo a specific training and expansion of consciousness. In turn these adepts and Masters had Their places filled by initiates, and thus constantly has there been opportunity for disciples and highly evolved men and women to pass into the ranks of the Hierarchy, and thus constantly has there been a circulation of new life and blood, and the coming in of those who belong to a particular period or age.

Some of the great names during the later periods are known to history, such as Shri Sankaracharya, Vyasa,

Mahommet, Jesus of Nazareth, and Krishna, down to those lesser initiates, Paul of Tarsus, Luther, and certain of the outstanding lights in European history. Always have these men and women been agents for the carrying out of race purpose, for the bringing about of group conditions, and for the furthering of the evolution of humanity. Sometimes they have appeared as beneficent forces, bringing peace and contentment with them. More often have they come as agents of destruction, breaking up the old forms of religion and of government in order that the life within the rapidly crystallising form might be set free and build for itself a newer and a better vehicle.

Much that is stated here is already well known, and has already been given out in the different occult books. Yet in the wise and careful enunciation of collected facts, and their correlation with that which may be new to some students, comes an eventual synthetic grasp of the great plan, and a wise uniform realisation as to the work of that great group of liberated souls who, in utter self-abnegation, stand silently behind the world panorama. Through the power of their will, the strength of their meditations, the wisdom of their plans, and the scientific knowledge of energy which is theirs, they direct those force currents, and control those form-building agencies which produce all that is seen and unseen, movable and immovable in the sphere of creation within the three worlds. This, coupled to their vast experience, is what fits them to be the agents for the distribution of the energy of the Planetary Logos.

As has already been stated, at the head of affairs, controlling each unit and directing all evolution, stands the KING, the Lord of the World, Sanat Kumara, the Youth of Endless Summers, and the Fountainhead of the Will, (showing forth as Love) of the Planetary Logos. Co-operating with Him as His advisers are three Personalities

called the Pratyeka Buddhas, or the Buddhas of Activity.
These four are the embodiment of active intelligent loving
will. They are the full flowering of the intelligence, having
achieved in an earlier solar system that which man is now
striving to perfect. In earlier cycles in this system They
began to demonstrate intelligent love, and from the standpoint of the average human being They are perfect love
and perfect intelligence, though from the standpoint of that
Existence Who embraces even our planetary scheme in His
body of manifestation, that love aspect is as yet but in
process of developing, and the will is only embryonic.
Another solar system will see the will aspect come to fruition,
as love will mature in this.

Standing around the Lord of the World, but withdrawn
and esoteric, are three more Kumaras, Who make the
seven of planetary manifestation. Their work is to us necessarily obscure. The three exoteric Buddhas, or Kumaras,
are the sumtotal of activity or planetary energy, and the
three esoteric Kumaras embody types of energy which as
yet are not in full demonstration upon our planet. Each
of these six Kumaras is a reflection of, and the distributing
agent for, the energy and force of one of the six other
Planetary Logoi, the remaining six spirits before the Throne.
Sanat Kumara alone, in this scheme, is self-sustaining and
self-sufficient, being the physical incarnation of one of the
Planetary Logoi, which one it is not permissible to state,
as this fact is one of the secrets of initiation. Through each
of Them passes the life force of one of the six rays, and in
considering Them one might sum up Their work and position as follows:—

1. They each embody one of the six types of energy,
   with the Lord of the World as the synthesiser and
   the embodier of the perfect seventh type, our planetary type.

2. They are each distinguished by one of the six colours, with the Lord of the World showing forth the full planetary colour, these six being subsidiary.

3. Their work is therefore concerned, not only with force distribution, but with the passing into our scheme from other planetary schemes, of Egos seeking earth experience.

4. Each of Them is in direct communication with one or another of the sacred planets.

5. According to astrological conditions, and according to the turning of the planetary wheel of life, so one or another of these Kumaras will be active. The three Buddhas of Activity change from time to time, and become in turn exoteric or esoteric as the case may be. Only the King persists steadily and watchfully in active physical incarnation.

Besides these main presiding Personalities in the Council Chamber at Shamballa, there is a group of four Beings Who are the representatives upon the planet of the four Maharajas, or the four Lords of Karma in the solar system, who are specifically concerned with the evolution at the present time of the human kingdom. These four are connected with:—

1. The distribution of karma, or human destiny, as it affects individuals, and through the individuals, the groups.

2. The care and tabulation of the akashic records. They are concerned with the Halls of Records, or with the "keeping of the book," as it is called in the Christian Bible; They are known in the Christian world as the recording angels.

3. The participation in solar councils. They alone have the right during the world cycle to pass beyond the periphery of the planetary scheme, and participate in the councils of the Solar Logos. Thus They are literally planetary mediators, representing our Planetary Logos and all that concerns Him in the greater scheme of which He is but a part.

Co-operating with these karmic Lords are the large groups of initiates and devas who occupy themselves with the right adjustment of:—

a. World karma,
b. Racial karma,
c. National karma,
d. Group karma,
e. Individual karma,

and who are responsible to the Planetary Logos for the correct manipulation of those forces and building agencies which bring in the right Egos on the different rays at the correct times and seasons.

With all these groups we have little concern, for they are contacted only by initiates of the third initiation, and by those of even more exalted rank.

The remaining personnel of the Hierarchy is divided into three main and four subsidiary groups, each of these groups, as will be seen by reference to the appended chart, being presided over by one of Those Whom we call the three Great Lords.

The work of the Manu.

The Manu presides over group one. He is called Vaivasvata Manu, and is the Manu of the fifth root-race. He is the ideal man or thinker, and sets the type for our Aryan race, having presided over its destinies since its inception nearly one hundred thousand years ago. Other Manus have come and gone and His place will be, in the relatively near future, taken by someone else. He will then pass on to other work of a more exalted kind. The Manu, or the prototype of the fourth root-race, works in close co-opera- tion with Him, and has His centre of influence in China. He is the second Manu that the fourth root-race has had, having taken the place of the earlier Manu at the time of the final stages of Atlantean destruction. He has remained to foster the development of the race type, and to bring about its final disappearance. The periods of office of all the Manus overlap, but there remains no representative of the third root-race upon the globe at this time. Vaivasvata Manu has His dwelling place in the Himalaya mountains, and has gathered around Him at Shigatse some of those immediately connected with Aryan affairs in India, Europe and America, and those who will later be concerned with the coming sixth root-race. The plans are pre- pared for ages ahead, centres of energy are formed thou- sands of years before they will be required, and in the wise fore-knowledge of these Divine Men nothing is left to sudden eventuation, but all moves in ordered cycles and under rule and law, though within karmic limitations.

The work of the Manu is largely concerned with gov- ernment, with planetary politics, and with the founding, direction, and dissolution of racial types and forms. To Him is committed the will and purpose of the Planetary Logos. He knows what is the immediate objective for this cycle of evolution over which He has to preside, and His work concerns itself with making that will an accomplished fact. He works in closer co-operation with the building devas than does His Brother, the Christ, for to Him is given the work of setting the race type, of segregating the groups out of which races will develop, of manipulating the forces which move the earth's crust, of raising and lowering continents, of directing the minds of statesmen everywhere so that racial government will proceed as desired, and conditions be brought about which will produce those needed for the fostering of any particular type. Such a work can now be seen demonstrating in North America and Australia.

The energy which flows through Him emanates from the head centre of the Planetary Logos, passing to Him through the brain of Sanat Kumara, Who focalises all the planetary energy within Himself. He works by the means of a dynamic meditation, conducted within the head centre, and produces His results through His perfect realisation of that which has to be accomplished, through a power to visualise that which must be done to bring about accomplishment, and through a capacity to transmit creative and destructive energy to those who are His assistants. And all this is brought about through the power of the enunciated sound.

The work of the World Teacher, the Christ.

Group two has the World Teacher for its presiding Head. He is that Great Being Whom the Christian calls the Christ; He is known also in the Orient as the Bodhisattva, and as the Lord Maitreya, and is the One looked for by the devout Mohammedan, under the name of the Iman Madhi. He it is Who has presided over the destinies of life since about 600 B.C. and He it is Who has come out among men before, and Who is again looked for. He is the great Lord of Love and of Compassion, just as his predecessor, the Buddha, was the Lord of Wisdom.

Through Him flows the energy of the second aspect, reaching Him direct from the heart centre of the Planetary Logos via the heart of Sanat Kumara. He works by means of a meditation centred within the heart. He is the World Teacher, the Master of the Masters, and the Instructor of the Angels, and to Him is committed the guidance of the spiritual destinies of men, and the development of the realisation within each human being that he is a child of God and a son of the Most High.

Just as the Manu is occupied with the providing of the type and forms through which consciousness can evolve and gather experience, thus making existence in its deepest sense possible, so the World Teacher directs that indwelling consciousness in its life or spirit aspect, seeking to energise it within the form so that, in due course of time, that form can be discarded and the liberated spirit return whence it came. Ever since He left the earth, as related with approximate accuracy in the Bible story (though with much error in detail) has He stayed with the sons of men; never has He really gone, but only in appearance, and in a physical body He can be found by those who know the way, dwelling in the Himalayas, and working in close co-operation with His two great Brothers, the Manu and the Mahachohan. Daily He pours out His blessing on the world, and daily He stands under the great pine in His garden at the sunset hour with hands uplifted in blessing over all those who truly and earnestly seek to aspire. To Him all seekers are known, and, though they may remain unaware of Him, the light which He pours forth stimulates their desire, fosters the spark of struggling life and spurs on the aspirant until the momentous day dawns when they stand face to face with the One Who by being "lifted up" (occultly understood) is drawing all men unto Himself as the Initiator of the sacred mysteries.

The work of the Lord of Civilisation, the Mahachohan.

Group three has as its Head the Mahachohan. His rule over the group persists for a longer period than that of His two Brothers, and He may hold office for the term of several root-races. He is the sumtotal of the intelligence aspect. The present Mahachohan is not the original one Who held the office at the founding of the Hierarchy in Lemurian days—it was then held by one of the Kumaras, or Lords of the Flame, Who came into incarnation with Sanat Kumara—but He took hold of His position during the second sub-race of the Atlantean root-race. He had achieved adeptship on the moon-chain, and it was through His instrumentality that a large number of the present more advanced human beings came into incarnation in the middle of the Atlantean root-race. Karmic affiliation with Him was one of the predisposing causes, thus making this eventuality possible.

His work concerns itself with the fostering and strengthening of that relation between spirit and matter, life and form, the self and the not-self, which results in what we call civilisation. He manipulates the forces of nature, and is largely the emanating source of electrical energy as we know it. Being the reflection of the third, or creative aspect, energy from the Planetary Logos flows to Him from the throat centre, and He it is Who in many ways makes the work of His Brothers possible. Their plans and desires are submitted to Him, and through Him pass the instructions to a large number of the deva agents.

Thus you have Will, Love, and Intelligence represented in these three great Lords; you have the self, the not-self, and the relation between synthesised in the unity of manifestation; you have racial government, religion and civilisation forming a coherent whole, and you have physical manifestation, the love or desire aspect, and the mind of the Planetary Logos working out into objectivity. The closest co-operation and unity exists between these three Personalities, and every move and plan and event exists in Their united foreknowledge. They are in daily touch with the Lord of the World at Shamballa, and the entire guidance of affairs rests in Their hands, and in those of the Manu of the fourth root-race. The World Teacher holds office in connection with both the fourth and fifth root-races.

Each of these departmental heads directs a number of subsidiary offices, and the department of the Mahachohan is divided into five divisions, so as to take in the four lesser aspects of Hierarchical rule.

Under the Manu work the regents of the different world divisions, such as, for instance, the Master Jupiter, the oldest of the Masters now working in physical bodies for humanity, Who is the regent for India, and the Master Rakoczi, Who is the regent for Europe and America. It must be remembered here that though the Master R., for instance, belongs to the seventh ray, and thus comes under the department of energy of the Mahachohan, yet in Hierarchical work He may and does hold office temporarily under the Manu. These regents hold in Their hands the reins of government for continents and nations, thus guiding, even if unknown, their destinies; They impress and inspire statesmen and rulers; They pour forth mental energy on governing groups, thus bringing about the desired results wherever co-operation and receptive intuition can be found amongst the thinkers.

The World Teacher presides over the destiny of the great religions through the medium of a group of Masters and initiates Who direct the activities of these different schools of thought. In illustration:—The Master Jesus, the inspirer and director of the Christian Churches everywhere, though an adept on the sixth ray under the department of the Mahachohan, works at present under the Christ for the welfare of Christianity; other Masters hold similar posts in relation to the great oriental faiths, and the various occidental schools of thought.

In the department of the Mahachohan a large number of Masters, in fivefold division, work in connection with the deva evolution, and with the intelligence aspect in man. Their divisions follow those of the four minor rays of attribute:—

1. The ray of harmony or beauty.
2. The ray of concrete science or knowledge.
3. The ray of devotion or abstract idealism.
4. The ray of ceremonial law or magic,

just as the three departmental heads represent the three major rays of:—

I. Will or power.
II. Love or wisdom.
III. Active intelligence, or adaptability.

The four rays or attributes of mind, with the third ray of intelligence, as synthesised by the Mahachohan, make up the sumtotal of the fifth principle of mind or manas.

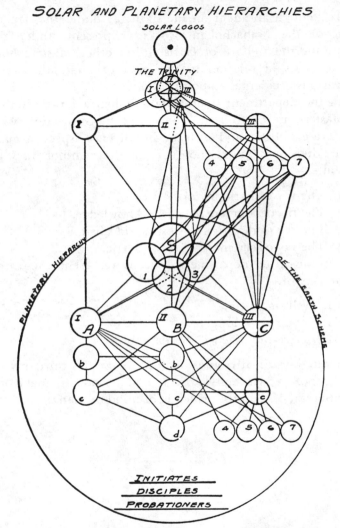

SOLAR AND PLANETARY HIERARCHIES

SOLAR LOGOS

THE TRINITY

PLANETARY HIERARCHY

OF THE EARTH SCHEME

INITIATES

DISCIPLES

PROBATIONERS

"This diagram is an outline of a portion of the Hierarchy at the present moment, and gives only the outstanding Figures, in connection with human evolution. A similar diagram from the standpoint of the deva evolution would be differently arranged." (The connecting lines indicate force currents)

48

KEY TO DIAGRAM OF SOLAR AND PLANETARY HIERARCHIES

THE SOLAR HIERARCHY

The Solar Logos.

The Solar Trinity or Logoi

I   The Father.......................Will.
II The Son................Love-Wisdom.
III The Holy Spirit....Active Intelligence.

The Seven Rays

Three Rays of Aspect.
Four Rays of Attribute.

I. Will or Power....II. Love-Wisdom....III. Active Intelligence

4. Harmony or Beauty.
5. Concrete Knowledge.
6. Devotion or Idealism.
7. Ceremonial Magic

THE PLANETARY HIERARCHY

S. Sanat Kumara, the Lord of the World.
(The Ancient of Days.
The One Initiator).

The Three Kumaras.
(The Buddhas of Activity.)
1   2   3

The reflections of the 3 major and 4 minor Rays.

The 3 Departmental Heads.

I. *The Will Aspect*.......	II. *The Love-Wisdom Aspect.*	III. *Intelligence Aspect.*
A. The Manu.	B. The Bodhisattva. (The Christ. The World Teacher.)	C. The Mahachohan. (Lord of Civilisation)
b. Master Jupiter.	b. A European Master.	
c. Master M—.	c. Master K.H.	c. The Venetian Master.
	d. Master D.K.	4. The Master Serapis. 5. Master Hilarion. 6. Master Jesus. 7. Master R—.

Four grades of initiates.

Various grades of disciples.

People on the Probationary Path.

Average humanity of all degrees.

CHAPTER VI

THE LODGE OF MASTERS

The divisions.

We have considered somewhat the highest offices in the ranks of the Hierarchy of our planet. Now we will deal with what we might call the two divisions into which the remaining members are divided. They form literally two Lodges within the greater body:—

a. The —— Lodge, comprised of initiates above the fifth initiation, and a group of devas or angels.

b. The Blue Lodge, comprised of all initiates of the third, fourth, and fifth initiations.

Below these come a large group of initiates of the first and second initiations, and then the disciples of every grade. The disciples are considered as affiliated with the Lodge, but not as literally members of it. Finally come those who are on probation, and who hope through strenuous effort to achieve affiliation.

From another point of view we can consider the Lodge members as existing in seven groups, each group representing one type of the sevenfold planetary energy emanating from the Planetary Logos. The triple division has first been given, as ever in evolution you have the major three (manifesting through the three departments) and then the seven, these seven showing again as a triple differentiation and a septenary. Students must bear in mind that all that is herein imparted concerns the work of the Hierarchy in connection with the fourth or human kingdom, and refers especially to those Masters Who work in connection with humanity. Were the deva evolution being dealt with, the entire tabulation and division would have to differ from this.

Again, there are certain aspects of hierarchical work affecting, for instance, the animal kingdom; this work calls into activity beings and workers and adepts totally distinct from the servers of the fourth or human kingdom. Therefore students should carefully remember that all these details are relative, and that the work and personnel of the Hierarchy are infinitely greater and more important than may appear upon a superficial reading of these pages. Certainly we are dealing with what might be considered Its primary work, for in the service of the human kingdom we are concerned with the manifestation of the three aspects of divinity, but the other departments are interdependent and the work progresses as a synthetic *whole*.

The workers, or adepts, concerned with the evolution of the human family, comprise sixty-three, if the three great Lords are counted in making the nine times seven necessary for the work. Of these forty-nine work exoterically, if it might be so expressed, and fourteen esoterically, being more concerned with the subjective manifestation. Not many of Their names are known to the public, nor would it be wise in many cases to reveal Who They are, where They dwell, and what is Their particular sphere of activity. A very small minority, through group karma and a willingness thus to sacrifice Themselves, have come before the public eye during the past one hundred years, and therefore concerning these, certain information may be given out. Quite a number of people in the world today are aware of Their existence independently of any particular school of thought, and the realisation that Those Whom they thus know personally are workers in a great and unified scheme of endeavour may encourage these real knowers to testify to their knowledge, and thus establish past all controversy the reality of Their work. Certain schools of occultism and of theosophical endeavour have claimed to be the sole repository of Their teaching, and the sole outlet for Their efforts, thereby limiting that which They do, and formulating premises which time and circumstance will fail to substantiate. They work most assuredly through such groups of thinkers, and throw much of Their force into the work of such organisations, yet, nevertheless, They have Their disciples and Their followers everywhere, and work through many bodies and many aspects of teaching. Throughout the world, disciples of these Masters have come into incarnation at this time with the sole intent of participating in the activities and occupations and truth dissemination of the various churches, sciences, and philosophies, and thus producing within the organisation itself an expansion, a widening, and a disintegration where necessary, which might otherwise be impossible. It might be wise for occult students everywhere to recognise these facts, and to cultivate the ability to recognise the hierarchical vibration as it demonstrates through the medium of disciples in the most unlikely places and groups.

One point should here be stated in connection with the work of the Masters through Their disciples, and it is this. All the various schools of thought which are fostered by the energy of the Lodge are, in every case, founded by a disciple, or several disciples, and upon these disciples, and not upon the Master, lies responsibility for results and the consequent karma. The method of procedure is somewhat as follows:— The Master reveals to a disciple the objective in view for an immediate little cycle, and suggests to him that such and such a development would be desirable. It is the work of the disciple to ascertain the best method for bringing about the desired results, and to for-mulate the plans whereby a certain percentage of success will be possible. Then he launches his scheme, founds his society or organisation, and disseminates the necessary teaching. Upon him rests the responsibility for choosing the right co-workers, for handing on the work to those best fitted, and for clothing the teaching in a presentable garb. All that the Master does is to look on with interest and sympathy at the endeavour, as long as it holds its initial high ideal and proceeds with pure altruism upon its way. The Master is not to blame should the disciple show lack of discrimination in the choice of co-workers, or evidence an inability to represent the truth. If he does well, and the work proceeds as desired, the Master will continue to pour His blessing upon the attempt. If he fails, or his successors turn from the original impulse, thus disseminating error of any kind, in His love and in His sympathy the Master will withdraw that blessing, withhold His energy, and thus cease from stimulating that which had better die. Forms may come and go, and the interest of the Master and His blessing pour through this or that channel; the work may proceed through one medium or another, but always the life force persists, shattering the form where it is inadequate, or utilising it when it suffices for the immediate need.

Certain Masters and Their Work.

Under the first great group of which the Manu is the Head, can be found two Masters, the Master Jupiter, and the Master Morya. Both of them have taken more than the fifth initiation, and the Master Jupiter, Who is also the Regent of India, is looked up to by all the Lodge of Masters as the oldest among Them. He dwells in the Nilgherry Hills in Southern India, and is not one of the Masters Who usually takes pupils, for He numbers amongst His disciples initiates of high degree and quite a number of Masters. In His hands are the reins of government for India, including a large part of the Northern frontier, and to Him is committed the arduous task of eventually guiding India out of her present chaos and unrest, and of welding her diverse peoples into an ultimate synthesis. The Master Morya, Who is one of the best known of the Eastern adepts, and Who numbers amongst His pupils a large number of Europeans and Americans, is a Rajput Prince, and for many decades held an authoritative position in Indian affairs.

He works in close co-operation with the Manu, and will Himself eventually hold office as the Manu of the sixth root-race. He dwells, as does His Brother, the Master K. H., at Shigatse in the Himalayas, and is a well-known figure to the inhabitants of that far-away village. He is a man of tall and commanding presence, dark hair and beard and dark eyes, and might be considered stern were it not for the expression that lies in His eyes. He and His Brother, the Master K. H., work almost as a unit, and have done so for many centuries and will, on into the future, for the Master K. H. is in line for the office of World Teacher when the present holder of that office vacates it for higher work, and the sixth root-race comes into being. The houses in which They both dwell are close together, and much of Their time is spent in the closest association. As the Master M. is upon the first Ray, that of Will or Power, His work largely concerns itself with the carrying out of the plans of the present Manu. He acts as the Inspirer of the statesmen of the world, He manipulates forces, through the Mahachohan, that will bring about the conditions desired for the furthering of racial evolution. On the physical plane those great national executives who have far vision and the international ideal are influenced by Him, and with Him co-operate certain of the great devas of the mental plane, and three great groups of angels work with Him on mental levels, in connection with the lesser devas who vitalise thoughtforms, and thus keep alive the thoughtforms of the Guides of the race for the benefit of the whole of humanity.

The Master M. has a large body of pupils under His instruction, and works in connection with many organisations of an esoteric and occult kind, as well as through the politicians and statesmen of the world.

The Master Koot Humi, Who is also very well known in the occident, and has many pupils everywhere, is of Kashmiri origin, though the family originally came from India. He is also an initiate of high degree, and is upon the second, or the Love-Wisdom Ray. He is a man of noble presence, and tall, though of rather slighter build than the Master M. He is of fair complexion, with golden-brown hair and beard, and eyes of a wonderful deep blue, through which seem to pour the love and the wisdom of the ages. He has had a wide experience and education, having been originally educated at one of the British universities, and speaks English fluently. His reading is wide and extensive, and all the current books and literature in various languages find their way to His study in the Himalayas. He concerns Himself largely with the vitalising of certain of the great philosophies, and interests Himself in a number of philanthropic agencies. To Him is given the work very largely of stimulating the love manifestation which is latent in the hearts of all men, and of awakening in the consciousness of the race the perception of the great fundamental fact of brotherhood.

At this particular time the Master M., the Master K. H. and the Master Jesus are interesting Themselves closely with the work of unifying, as far as may be, eastern and western thought, so that the great religions of the East, with the later development of the Christian faith in all its many branches, may mutually benefit each other. Thus eventually it is hoped one great universal Church may come into being.

The Master Jesus, Who is the focal point of the energy that flows through the various Christian churches, is at present living in a Syrian body, and dwells in a certain part of the Holy Land. He travels much and passes considerable time in various parts of Europe. He works specially with masses more than with individuals, though He has gathered around Him quite a numerous body of pupils. He is upon the sixth Ray of Devotion, or Abstract Idealism, and His pupils are frequently distinguished by that fanaticism and devotion which manifested in earlier Christian times amongst the martyrs. He Himself is rather a martial figure, a disciplinarian, and a man of iron rule and will. He is tall and spare with rather a long thin face, black hair, pale complexion and piercing blue eyes. His work at this time is exceedingly responsible, for to Him is given the problem of steering the thought of the occident out of its present state of unrest into the peaceful waters of certitude and knowledge, and of preparing the way in Europe and America for the eventual coming of the World Teacher. He is well known in the Bible history, coming before us first as Joshua the Son of Nun, appearing again in the time of Ezra as Jeshua, taking the third initiation, as related in the book of Zechariah, as Joshua, and in the Gospel story He is known for two great sacrifices, that in which He handed over His body for the use of the Christ, and for the great renunciation which is the characteristic of the fourth initiation. As Appollonius of Tyana, He took the fifth initiation and became a Master of the Wisdom. From that time on He has stayed and worked with the Christian Church, fostering the germ of true spiritual life which is to be found amongst members of all sects and divisions, and neutralising as far as possible the mistakes and errors of the churchmen and the theologians. He is distinctively the Great Leader, the General, and the wise Executive, and in Church matters He co-operates closely with the Christ, thus saving Him much and acting as His intermediary wherever possible. No one so wisely knows as He the problems of the West, no one is so closely in touch with the people who stand for all that is best in Christian teachings, and no one is so well aware of the need of the present moment. Certain great prelates of the Anglican and Catholic Churches are wise agents of His.

The Master Djwhal Khul, or the Master D. K. as He is frequently called, is another adept on the second Ray of Love-Wisdom. He is the latest of the adepts taking initiation, having taken the fifth initiation in 1875, and is therefore occupying the same body in which He took the initiation, most of the other Masters having taken the fifth initiation whilst occupying earlier vehicles. His body is not a young one, and He is a Tibetan. He is very devoted to the Master K. H. and occupies a little house not far distant from the larger one of the Master, and from His willingness to serve and to do anything that has to be done, He has been called "the Messenger of the Masters." He is profoundly learned, and knows more about the rays and planetary Hierarchies of the solar system than anyone else in the ranks of the Masters. He works with those who heal, and co-operates unknown and unseen with the seekers after truth in the world's great laboratories, with all who definitely aim at the healing and solacing of the world, and with the great philanthropic world movements such as the Red Cross. He occupies Himself with various pupils of different Masters who can profit by His instruction, and within the last ten years has relieved both the Master M. and the Master K. H. of a good deal of Their teaching work, taking over from Them for certain stated times some of Their pupils and disciples. He works largely, too, with certain groups of the devas of the ethers, who are the healing devas, and who thus collaborate with Him in the work of healing some of the physical ills of humanity. He it was Who dictated a large part of that momentous book The Secret Doctrine, and Who showed to H. P. Blavatsky many of the pictures, and gave her much of the data that is to be found in that book.

The Master Who concerns Himself especially with the future development of racial affairs in Europe, and with the mental outgrowth in America and Australia, is the Master Rakoczi. He is a Hungarian, and has a home in the Carpathian mountains, and was at one time a well-known figure at the Hungarian Court. Reference to Him can be found in old historical books, and He was particularly before the public eye when he was the Comte de St. Germain, and earlier still when he was both Roger Bacon and later, Francis Bacon. It is interesting to note that as the Master R. takes hold, on the inner planes, of affairs in Europe, His name as Francis Bacon is coming before the public eye in the Bacon-Shakespeare controversy. He is rather a small, spare man, with pointed black beard, and smooth black hair, and does not take as many pupils as do the Masters previously mentioned. He is at present handling the majority of the third ray pupils in the occident in conjunction with the Master Hilarion. The Master R. is upon the seventh Ray, that of Ceremonial Magic or Order, and He works largely through esoteric ritual and ceremonial, being vitally interested in the effects, hitherto unrecognised, of the ceremonial of the Freemasons, of the various fraternities and of the Churches everywhere. He is called in the Lodge, usually, "the Count," and in America and Europe acts practically as the general manager for the carrying out of the plans of the executive council of the Lodge. Certain of the Masters form around the three great Lords an inner group, and meet in council with great frequency.

On the fifth Ray of Concrete Knowledge or Science, we find the Master Hilarion, who, in an earlier incarnation was Paul of Tarsus. He is occupying a Cretan body, but spends a large part of His time in Egypt. He it was Who gave out to the world that occult treatise "Light on the Path," and His work is particularly interesting to the general public at this crisis, for He works with those who are developing the intuition, and controls and transmutes the great movements that tend to strip the veil from the unseen. His is the energy which, through His disciples, is stimulating the Psychical Research groups everywhere, and He it was Who initiated, through various pupils of His, the Spiritualistic movement. He has under observation all those who are psychics of the higher or-der, and assists in developing their powers for the good of the group, and in connection with certain of the devas of the astral plane He works to open up to the seekers after truth that subjective world which lies behind the grossly material.

Little can be given out anent the two English Mas-ters. Neither of them takes pupils in the same sense that the Master K. H. or the Master M. take pupils. One of Them, who resides in Great Britain, has in hand the definite guidance of the Anglo-Saxon race, and He works upon the plans for its future development and evolution. He is behind the Labour movement throughout the world, transmuting and directing, and the present rising tide of democracy has His directing hand upon it. Out of the democratic unrest, out of the present turmoil and chaos, will arise the future world condition which will have for its keynote co-operation and not competition, distribution, and not centralisation.

One other Master may here be briefly mentioned, the Master Serapis, frequently called the Egyptian. He is the Master upon the fourth ray, and the great art movements of the world, the evolution of music, and that of painting and drama, receive from Him an energising impulse. At present He is giving most of His time and attention to the work of the deva, or angel evolution, until their agency helps to make possible the great revelation in the world of music and painting which lies immediately ahead. More about Him cannot be given out, nor can His dwelling place be revealed.

The Master P. works under the Master R. in North America. He it is Who has had much to do esoterically with the various mental sciences, such as Christian Science, and New Thought, both of which are efforts put forth by the Lodge in an endeavour to teach men the reality of that which is not seen, and the power of the mind to create. This Master occupies an Irish body, is on the fourth ray, and the place of His residence may not be revealed. Much of the work of the Master Serapis was taken over by Him when the latter turned His attention to the deva evolution.

The present work.

Certain facts concerning these Masters, and Their work in the present and in the future, may be in place here. First, the work of training Their pupils and disciples to fit them to be of use in two great events, one, the coming of the World Teacher towards the middle or close of this present century, and the other, the training of them to be of use in the founding of the new sixth sub-race and in the reconstruction of the present world conditions. This being the fifth sub-race of the fifth root-race, the pressure of the work on the five rays of mind which are controlled by the Mahachohan, is very great. The Masters are carrying an over heavy burden, and much of Their work of teaching disciples has been delegated to initiates and advanced disciples, and certain of the Masters on the first and second rays have temporarily taken over pupils in the Mahachohan's department.

Secondly, the preparation of the world on a large scale for the coming of the World Teacher, and the taking of the necessary steps before They Themselves come out among men, as many of Them surely will towards the close of this century. A special group is forming amongst Them now Who are definitely preparing Themselves for this work. The Master M., the Master K. H. and the Master Jesus will be specially concerned with the movement towards the last quarter of this century. Other Masters will participate also, but these three are the ones with Whose names and offices people should familiarise themselves, wherever possible. Two other Masters, specially concerned with the seventh or ceremonial ray, Whose particular work it is to supervise the development of certain activities within the next fifteen years, work under the Master R. Very definitely may the assurance be given here, that prior to the coming of the Christ, adjustments will be made so that at the head of all great organisations will be found either a Master, or an initiate who has taken the third initiation. At the head of certain of the great occult groups, of the Freemasons of the world, and of the various great divisions of the Church, and resident in many of the great nations will be found initiates or Masters. This work of the Masters is proceeding now, and all Their efforts are being bent towards bringing it to a successful consummation. Everywhere They are gathering in those who in any way show a tendency to respond to high vibration, seeking to force their vibration and to fit them so that they may be of use at the time of the coming of the Christ. Great is the day of opportunity, for when that time comes, through the stupendous strength of the vibration then brought to bear upon the sons of men, it will be possible for those who now do the necessary work to take a great step forward, and to pass through the portal of initiation.

CHAPTER VII

THE PROBATIONARY PATH

Preparation for Initiation.

The Probationary Path precedes the Path of Initiation or Holiness, and marks that period in the life of a man when he definitely sets himself on the side of the forces of evolution, and works at the building of his own character. He takes himself in hand, cultivates the qualities that are lacking in his disposition, and seeks with diligence to bring his personality under control. He is building the causal body with deliberate intent, filling any gaps that may exist, and seeking to make it a fit receptacle for the Christ principle. The analogy between the prenatal period in the history of the human being and that of the development of the indwelling spirit is curiously interesting. We might look at it in this way:—

1. The moment of conception, corresponding to that of individualisation.
2. Nine months' gestation, corresponding to the wheel of life.
3. The first initiation, corresponding to the birth hour.

The Probationary Path corresponds to the latter period of gestation, to the building in the heart of the babe in Christ. At the first initiation this babe starts on the pilgrimage of the Path. The first initiation stands simply for commencement. A certain structure of right living, thinking, and conduct has been built up. That form we call character. It has now to be vivified and indwelt. Thackeray has well described this process of building, in the words so often quoted:—

"Sow a thought and reap an action; sow an action
and reap a habit; sow a habit and reap character;
sow character and reap destiny."

The immortal destiny of each and all of us is to attain the
consciousness of the higher self, and subsequently that of
the Divine Spirit. When the form is ready, when Solomon's temple has been built in the quarry of the personal
life, then the Christ-life enters, and the glory of the Lord
overshadows His temple. The form becomes vibrant.
Therein lies the difference between theory and making
that theory part of oneself. One can have a perfect image
or picture, but it lacks life. The life can be modelled on
the divine as far as may be; it may be an excellent copy
but lacks the indwelling Christ principle. The germ has
been there, but it has lain dormant. Now it is fostered
and brought to the birth and the first initiation is attained.

Whilst the man is on the Probationary Path he is
taught principally to know himself, to ascertain his weak-
nesses and to correct them. He is taught to work as an
invisible helper at first and for several lives is generally
kept at this kind of work. Later, as he makes progress,
he may be moved to more selected work. He is taught the
rudiments of the Divine Wisdom and is entered into the
final grades in the Hall of Learning. He is known to a
Master, and is in the care (for definite teaching) of one
of the disciples of that Master, or, if of rare promise, of
an initiate.

Classes are held by initiates of the first and second
degrees, for accepted disciples and those on probation, between the hours of ten and five every night in all parts of
the world, so that the continuity of the teaching is complete. They gather in the Hall of Learning and the method
is much the same as in the big Universities,—classes at
certain hours, experimental work, examinations, and a

gradual moving up and onward as the tests are passed. A number of the Egos on the Probationary Path are in the department that is analogous to the High School; others have matriculated and are in the University itself. Graduation results when initiation is taken and the initiate passes into the Hall of Wisdom.

Advanced Egos and the spiritually inclined, who are not yet on the Probationary Path, attend instructions from disciples, and on occasions large classes are conducted for their benefit by initiates. Their work is more rudimentary, though occult from a worldly standpoint, and they learn under supervision to be invisible helpers. The invisible helpers are usually recruited from amongst the advanced Egos. The very advanced, and those on the Probationary Path and nearing initiation, work more frequently in what might be termed departmental work, forming a group of assistants to the Members of the Hierarchy.

Methods of teaching.

Three departments of instruction watch over three parts of man's development.

First: Instruction is given tending to the disciplining of the life, the growth of character, the development of the microcosm along cosmic lines. The man is taught the meaning of himself; he comes to know himself as a complex, complete unit, a replica in miniature of the outer world. In learning the laws of his own being, comes comprehension of the Self, and a realisation of the basic laws of the system.

Secondly: Instruction is given as to the macrocosm, the amplification of his intellectual grip of the working of the cosmos. Information as to the kingdoms of nature, teaching as to the laws of those kingdoms, and instruction as to the working of those laws in all kingdoms and on all planes is given him. He acquires a deep fund of general knowledge, and when he reaches his own periphery he is met by those who lead him on to encyclopaedic knowledge. When he has attained the goal, he may not know every single thing that there is to be known in all the three worlds, but the way to know, the sources of knowledge and the reservoirs of information are in his hand. A Master can at any time find out anything on any possible subject without the slightest difficulty.

Thirdly: Instruction is given in what might be termed *synthesis*. This information is only possible as the intuitional vehicle co-ordinates. It is really the occult apprehension of the law of gravitation or attraction, (the basic law of this, the second solar system) with all its corollaries. The disciple learns the meaning of occult cohesion, and of that internal unity which holds the system as a homogeneous unit. The major part of this instruction is usually given after the third initiation, but a beginning is made early in the training.

Masters and disciples.

Disciples and advanced Egos on the Probationary Path receive instruction at this particular time for two special purposes:—

(a) To test out their fitness for special work lying in the future, the type of that work being known only to the Guides of the race. They are tested for aptitude in community living with a view to drafting the suitable ones into the colony of the sixth sub-race. They are tested for various lines of work, many incomprehensible to us now, but which will become ordinary methods of development as time progresses. The Masters also test for those in whom the intuition has reached a point of development that indicates a beginning of the co-ordination of the buddhic vehicle, or—to be exact—has reached a point where molecules of the seventh sub-plane of the buddhic plane can be discerned in the aura of the Ego. When this is so They can go ahead with confidence in the work of instruction, knowing that certain imparted facts will be understood.

(b) Instruction is being given at this time to a special group of people who have come into incarnation at this critical period of the world's history. They have come in, all at the same time, throughout the world, to do the work of *linking up the two planes, the physical and astral, via the etheric.*

This sentence is for serious consideration, for it covers the work that a number of the newer generation have come to do. In this linking up of the two planes people are required who are polarised in their mental bodies (or, if not polarised there, are nevertheless well rounded out and balanced) and can therefore work safely and with intelligence in this type of work. It necessitates primarily people in whose vehicles can be found a certain proportion of atomic sub-plane matter, so that direct communication can be effected between the higher and the lower via the atomic cross-section of the causal body. This is not easy to explain clearly, but a consideration of the diagram in "A Study in Consciousness," by Mrs. Besant, page 27, may be helpful in explaining some matters that are apt to puzzle.

We must recognise two things in pondering the subject of the Masters and Their disciples. First, that in the Hierarchy nothing is lost through failure to recognise the law of economy. Every expenditure of force on the part of a Master or Teacher is subjected to wise foresight and discrimination. Just as we do not put university professors to teach the beginners, so the Masters Themselves work not individually with men until they have attained a certain stage of evolution and are ready to profit by Their instruction.

Secondly, we must remember that each of us is recognised by the brilliance of his light. This is an occult fact. The finer the grade of matter built into our bodies, the more brilliantly will shine forth the indwelling light. Light is vibration, and through the measurement of vibration is fixed the grading of the scholars. Hence nothing can prevent a man's progress forward if he but attends to the purification of his vehicles. The light within will shine forth with ever greater clarity, as the refining process goes on, until—when atomic matter predominates—great will be the glory of that inner man. We are all graded, therefore, if it may be so expressed, according to the magnitude of the light, according to the rate of vibration, according to the purity of the tone and the clarity of the colour. Who our Teacher is depends therefore upon our grading. Similarity of vibration holds the secret. We are frequently told that when the demand is forceful enough the Teacher will appear. When we build in the right vibrations and attune ourselves to the right key, nothing can prevent our finding the Master.

Groups of Egos are formed:—

1. According to their ray.
2. According to their sub-ray.
3. According to their rate of vibration.

They are also grouped for purposes of classification:

1. As Egos, according to the egoic ray.
2. As personalities, according to the sub-ray which is governing the personality.

All are graded and charted. The Masters have Their Halls of Records, with a system of tabulation incomprehensible to us owing to its magnitude and its necessary intricacies, wherein these charts are kept. They are under the care of a Chohan of a Ray, each ray having its own collection of charts. These charts, being in many sec‹ tions (dealing with incarnate, discarnate, and perfected Egos), are again all under the care of subordinate guardians. The Lipika Lords, with Their vast band of helpers are the most frequent users of these charts. Many discarnate egos awaiting incarnation or having just left the earth, sacrifice their time in heaven to assist in this work. These Halls of Records are mostly on the lowest levels of the mental plane and the highest of the astral, as they can be there most fully utilised and are most easily accessible.

Initiates receive instruction directly from the Masters or from some of the great devas or angels. These teachings are usually imparted at night in small classes, or individually (should the occasion warrant it) in the Master's private study. The above applies to initiates in incarnation or on the inner planes. If on causal levels, they receive instruction at any time deemed advisable direct from the Master to the Ego on causal levels.

Disciples are taught in groups in the Master's ashram, or classroom, at night, if in incarnation. Apart from these regular gatherings, in order to receive direct teaching from the Master, a disciple (for some specific reason) may be called to the Master's study for a private interview. This occurs when a Master wishes to see a disciple for commendation, warning, or to decide if initiation is desirable. The major part of a disciple's tuition is left in the hands of some initiate or more advanced disciple, who watches over his younger brother, and is responsible to the Master for his progress, handing in regular reports. Karma is largely the arbiter of this relation.

Just at present, owing to the great need in the world, a slightly different policy is being pursued. An intensified training is being given to some disciples by some Masters

Who have not hitherto taken pupils. The press of work on the Masters Who do take disciples being so great, They have delegated some of Their most promising pupils to some other Masters, drafting them into small groups for a brief period. The experiment is being tried of intensifying the teaching, and of subjecting disciples, not initiates, to the frequent strong vibration of a Master. It involves risk, but, if the experiment proves successful, will tend to the greater assisting of the race.

CHAPTER VIII

DISCIPLESHIP

A disciple described.

A disciple is one who above all else, is pledged to do three things:—

a. To serve humanity.
b. To co-operate with the plan of the Great Ones as he sees it and as best he may.
c. To develop the powers of the Ego, to expand his consciousness until he can function on the three planes in the three worlds, and in the causal body, and to follow the guidance of the higher self and not the dictates of his three-fold lower manifestation.

A disciple is one who is beginning to comprehend group work, and to change his centre of activity from himself (as the pivot around which everything revolves) to the group centre.

A disciple is one who realises simultaneously the relative insignificance of each unit of consciousness, and also its vast importance. His sense of proportion is adjusted, and he sees things as they are; he sees people as they are; he sees himself as he inherently is and seeks then to become that which he is.

A disciple realises the life or force side of nature, and to him the form makes no appeal. He works with force and through force; he recognises himself as a force centre within a greater force centre, and his is the responsibility of directing the energy which may pour through him into channels through which the group can be benefited.

The disciple knows himself to be—to a greater or less degree—an outpost of the Master's consciousness, viewing the Master in a two-fold sense:—

a. As his own egoic consciousness.
b. As the centre of his group; the force animating the units of the group and binding them into a homogeneous whole.

A disciple is one who is transferring his consciousness out of the personal into the impersonal, and during the transition stage much of difficulty and of suffering is necessarily endured. These difficulties arise from various causes:—

a. The disciple's lower self, which rebels at being transmuted.
b. A man's immediate group, friends, or family, who rebel at his growing impersonality. They do not like to be acknowledged as one with him on the life side, and yet separate from him where desires and interests lie. Yet the law holds good, and only in the essential life of the soul can true unity be cognised. In the discovery as to what is form lies much of sorrow for the disciple, but the road leads to perfect union eventually.

The disciple is one who realises his responsibility to all units who come under his influence,—a responsibility of co-operating with the plan of evolution as it exists for them, and thus to expand their consciousness and teach them the difference between the real and the unreal, between life and form. This he does most easily by a demonstration in his own life as to his goal, his object, and his centre of consciousness.

The work to be done.

The disciple, therefore, has several things at which to aim:—

A sensitive response to the Master's vibration.

A practical purity of life; a purity not merely theoretical.

A freedom from care. Here bear in mind that care is based on the personal, and is the result of lack of dispassion and a too ready response to the vibrations of the lower worlds.

Accomplishment of duty. This point involves the dispassionate discharge of all obligations and due attention to karmic debts. Special emphasis should be laid, for all disciples, on the value of dispassion. Lack of discrimination is not so often a hindrance to disciples these days, owing to the development of the mind, but lack of dispassion frequently is. This means the attainment of that state of consciousness where balance is seen, and neither pleasure nor pain dominates, for they are superseded by joy and bliss. We may well ponder on this, for much striving after dispassion is necessary.

He has also to study the Kama-manasic body (desiremind body). This is of very real interest, for it is, in many ways, the most important body in the solar system, where the human being in the three worlds is concerned. In the next system the mental vehicle of the self-conscious units will hold an analogous place, as the physical did in the previous solar system.

He has also to work scientifically, if it may be so expressed, at the building of the physical body. He must so strive that he will produce in each incarnation a body which will serve better as a vehicle for force. Hence there is nothing impractical in giving information anent initiation, as some may think. There is no moment of the day that that goal may not be visioned, and the work of preparation carried on. One of the greatest instruments for practical development lying in the hands of small and great, is the instrument of SPEECH. He who guards his words, and who only speaks with altruistic purpose, in order to carry the energy of Love through the medium of the tongue, is one who is mastering rapidly the initial steps to be taken in preparation for initiation. Speech is the most occult manifestation in existence; it is the means of creation and the vehicle for force. In the reservation of words, esoterically understood, lies the conservation of force; in the utilisation of words, justly chosen and spoken, lies the distribution of the love force of the solar system,—that force which preserves, strengthens, and stimulates. Only he who knows somewhat of these two aspects of speech can be trusted to stand before the Initiator and to carry out from that Presence certain sounds and secrets imparted to him under the pledge of silence.

The disciple must learn to be silent in the face of that which is evil. He must learn to be silent before the sufferings of the world, wasting no time in idle plaints and sorrowful demonstration, but lifting up the burden of the world; working, and wasting no energy in talk. Yet withal he should speak where encouragement is needed, using the tongue for constructive ends; expressing the love force of the world, as it may flow through him, where it will serve best to ease a load or lift a burden, remembering that as the race progresses, the love element between the sexes and its expression will be translated to a higher plane. Then, through the spoken word, and not through the physical plane expression as now, will come the realisation of that true love which unites those who are one in service and in aspiration. Then love between the units of the human family will take the form of the utilisation of speech for the purpose of creating on all planes, and the energy which now, in the majority, finds expression through the lower or generating centres will be translated to the throat centre. This is as yet but a distant ideal, but even now some can vision that ideal, and seek—through united service, loving co-operation, and oneness in aspiration, thought, and endeavour,—to give shape and form to it, even though inadequately.

Group relationships.

The path of the disciple is a thorny one; briars beset his every step, and difficulties meet him at every turn. Yet in the treading of the path, in the overcoming of the difficulties, and in a single-hearted adherence to the good of the group, with a proportionate attention to the individuals and their evolutionary development, comes at length fruition, and the attainment of the goal. A SERVER of the race stands forth. He is a server because he has no ends of his own to serve, and from his lower sheaths goes out no vibration which can beguile him from his chosen path. He serves, because he knows what is in man, and because for many lives he has worked with individuals and with groups, gradually expanding the range of his endeavour until he has gathered around him those units of consciousness whom he can energise, and use, and through whom he can work out the plans of his superiors. Such is the goal, but the intermediate stages are fraught with difficulty for all who stand on the verge of self-discovery, and of becoming the Path itself.

Some practical advice might be of value here:—

Study with care the first three books of the Bhagavad Gita. The problem of Arjuna is the problem of all disciples, and the solution is eternally the same.

Stand ready and watch the heart. In the transferring of the fire from the solar plexus to the heart centre comes much pain. It is not easy to love as do the Great Ones, with a pure love which requires nothing back; with an impersonal love that rejoices where there is response, but looks not for it, and loves steadily, quietly, and deeply through all apparent divergences, knowing that when each has found his own way home, he will find that home to be the place of at-one-ment.

Be prepared for loneliness. It is the law. As a man dissociates himself from all that concerns his physical, astral and mental bodies, and centres himself in the Ego, it produces a temporary separation. This must be endured and passed, leading to a closer link at a later period with all associated with the disciple through the karma of past lives, through group work, and through the activity of the disciple (carried on almost unconsciously at first) in gathering together those through whom later he will work.

Cultivate happiness, knowing that depression, an over-morbid investigation of motive, and undue sensitiveness to the criticism of others leads to a condition wherein a disciple is almost useless. Happiness is based on confidence in the God within, a just appreciation of time, and a forgetfulness of self. Take all the glad things which may come as trusts to be used to spread joy, and rebel not at happiness and pleasure in service, thinking it an indication that all is not well. Suffering comes as the lower self rebels. Control that lower self, eliminate desire, and all is joy.

Have patience. Endurance is one of the characteristics of the Ego. The Ego *persists,* knowing itself immortal. The personality becomes discouraged, knowing that time is short.

To the disciple naught occurs but what is in the plan, and where the motive and sole aspiration of the heart are towards the carrying out of the Master's will and the serving of the race, that which eventuates has in it the seeds of the next enterprise, and embodies the environment of the next step forward. Herein lies much of clarification, and herein may be found that on which the disciple may rest when the vision is clouded, the vibration lower than perhaps it should be, and the judgment fogged by the miasmas arising from circumstances on the physical plane. With many, much arises in the astral body that is based on old vibration and has no foundation in fact, and the battleground is so to control the astral situation that out of present anxieties and worries may grow confidence and peace, and out of violent action and interaction there may be elaborated tranquility.

It is possible to reach a point where naught that occurs can ruffle the inner calm; where the peace that passeth understanding is known and experienced, because the consciousness is centred in the Ego, who is peace itself, being the circle of the buddhic life; where poise itself is known and felt, and equilibrium reigns because the centre of the life is in the Ego, who is—in essence—balance; where calm rules unruffled and unshaken, because the divine Knower holds the reins of government, and permits no disturbance from the lower self; where bliss itself is reached that is based, not on circumstances in the three worlds, but on that inner realisation of existence apart from the not-self, an existence that persists when time and space and all that is contained therein, are not; that is known when all the illusions of the lower planes are experienced, passed through, transmuted and transcended; that endures when the little world of human endeavour has dissipated and gone, being

seen as naught; and that is based on the knowledge that
I AM THAT.

Such an attitude and experience is for all those who
persist in their high endeavour, who count all things but
naught if they may but achieve the goal, and who steer a
steady course through circumstances, keeping the eyes fixed
upon the vision ahead, the ears attentive to the Voice of
the God within, that sounds in the silence of the heart;
the feet firmly placed on the path that leads to the Portal
of Initiation; the hands held out in assistance to the world,
and the whole life subordinated to the call of service. Then
all that comes is for the best—sickness, opportunity, success, and disappointment, the gibes and machinations of
enemies, the lack of comprehension on the part of those
we love—all is but to be used, and all exists but to be transmuted. Continuity of vision, of aspiration, and of the inner
touch, is seen to be of more importance than them all.
That continuity is the thing to be aimed at, in spite of, and
not because of circumstances.

As the aspirant progresses he not only balances the
pairs of opposites, but is having the secret of his brother's
heart revealed to him. He becomes an acknowledged force
in the world and is recognised as one who can be depended
upon to serve. Men turn to him for assistance and help
along his recognised line, and he begins to sound forth his
note so as to be heard in deva and human ranks. This he
does—at this stage—through the pen in literature, through
the spoken word in lecturing and teaching, through music,
painting and art. He reaches the hearts of men in some
way or another, and becomes a helper and server of his
race. Two more characteristics of this stage might here be
mentioned:—

The aspirant has an appreciation of the occult value
of money in service. He seeks nothing for himself, save

that which may equip him for the work to be done, and he looks upon money and that which money can purchase as something which is to be used for others and as a means to bring about the fruition of the Master's plans as he senses those plans. The occult significance of money is little appreciated, yet one of the greatest tests as to the position of a man upon the Probationary Path is that which concerns his attitude to and his handling of that which all men seek in order to gratify desire. Only he who desires naught for himself can be a recipient of financial bounty, and a dispenser of the riches of the universe. In other cases where riches increase they bring with them naught but sorrow and distress, discontent, and misuse.

At this stage also the aspirant's life becomes an instrument of destruction in the occult sense of the term. Wherever he goes the force which flows through him from the higher planes and his own inner God produces at times peculiar results upon his environment. It acts as a stimulator of both the good and the evil. The lunar Pitris, or little lives which form the bodies of his brother and his own body, are likewise stimulated, their activity is increased and their power greatly aggravated. This fact is used by Those Who work on the inner side to bring about certain desired ends. This it is also which often causes the temporary downfall of advanced souls. They cannot stand the force pouring into them, or upon them, and through the temporary over-stimulation of their centres and vehicles they go to pieces. This can be seen working out in groups as well as in individuals. But, inversely, if the lunar Lords, or lives of the lower self, have been earlier subjugated and brought under control, then the effect of the force and energy contacted is to stimulate the response of the physical brain consciousness and the head centres to egoic contact.

Then the otherwise destructive force becomes a factor for good and a helpful stimulation, and can be used by Those Who know how, to lead men on to further illumination.

All these steps have to work out on all the three lower planes, and in the three bodies, and this they do according to the particular ray and sub-ray. In this fashion is the work of the disciple carried forward, and his testing and training carried out. Thus is he brought—through right direction of energy and wise manipulation of force currents—to the Portal of Initiation, and he graduates from the Hall of Learning into the Hall of Wisdom, that Hall wherein he gradually becomes "aware" of forces and powers latent in his own Ego and egoic group, wherein the force of the egoic group is his for the using, for he can now be trusted to wield it only for the helping of humanity, and wherein—after the fourth initiation—he becomes a sharer in, and can be trusted with, some part of the energy of the Planetary Logos, and thus be enabled to carry forward the plans of that Logos for evolution.

It would be well to remember that disciples on the first ray understand discipleship largely in terms of energy, or force, or activity, whilst disciples on the second ray understand it more in terms of consciousness or initiation. Hence the divergence of expressions in ordinary use, and the lack of comprehension among thinkers. It might prove useful to express the idea of discipleship in terms of the different rays—meaning by this, discipleship as it manifests on the physical plane in service:

1st Ray...Force	Energy	Action	The Occultist.
2nd Ray..Consciousness	Expansion	Initiation	The true Psychic.
3rd Ray..Adaptation	Development	Evolution	The Magician.
4th Ray..Vibration	Response	Expression	The Artist.
5th Ray..Mentation	Knowledge	Science	The Scientist.
6th Ray..Devotion	Abstraction	Idealism	The Devotee.
7th Ray..Incantation	Magic	Ritual	The Ritualist.

Remember carefully that we are here dealing with disciples. Later on as they progress, the various lines approximate and merge. All have been at one time magicians, for all have passed upon the third ray. The problem now is concerned with the mystic and the occultist, and their eventual synthesis. A careful study of the foregoing will lead to the realisation that the difficulties between thinkers, and between disciples of all groups, consist in their identifying themselves with some form, and in their inability to understand the different points of view of others. As time elapses, and they are brought into closer relationship with the two Masters with whom they are concerned (their own inner God and their personal Master), the inability to co-operate and to merge their interests in the good of the group will pass away, and community of endeavour, similarity of object, and mutual co-operation will take the place of what is now so much seen, divergence. We might well ponder on this, for it holds the key to much that is puzzling and, to many, distressing.

CHAPTER IX

THE PATH OF INITIATION

After a longer or shorter period of time the disciple stands at the Portal of Initiation. We must remember that as one approaches this portal and draws nearer to the Master it is, as says "Light on the Path," with the feet bathed in the blood of the heart. Each step up is ever through the sacrifice of all that the heart holds dear on one plane or another, and always must this sacrifice be voluntary. He who treads the Probationary Path and the Path of Holiness is he who has counted the cost, whose sense of values has been readjusted, and who therefore judges not as judges the man of the world. He is the man who is attempting to take the "kingdom by violence," and in the attempt is prepared for the consequent suffering. He is the man who counts all things but loss if he may but win the goal, and who, in the struggle for the mastery of the lower self by the higher, is willing to sacrifice even unto death.

The first two initiations.

At the first initiation, the control of the Ego over the physical body must have reached a high degree of attainment. "The sins of the flesh," as the Christian phraseology has it, must be dominated; gluttony, drink, and licentiousness must no longer hold sway. The physical elemental will no longer find its demand obeyed; the control must be complete and the lure departed. A general attitude of obedience to the Ego must have been achieved, and the *willingness* to obey must be very strong. The channel between the higher and the lower is widened, and the obedience of the flesh practically automatic.

That all initiates measure not up to this standard may be ascribed to several things, but the note they sound should be on the side of righteousness; the recognition of their own shortcomings which they will evidence will be sincere and public, and their struggle to conform to the highest standard will be known, even though perfection may not be achieved. Initiates may, and do, fall, and thereby incur the working of the law in punishment. They may, and do, by this fall injure the group, and thereby incur the karma of readjustment, having to expiate the injury through later prolonged service, wherein the group members themselves, even though unconsciously, apply the law; their progress will be seriously hindered, much time being lost in which they must work out the karma with the injured units. The very fact that a man is an initiate, and therefore the medium for force of a greatly increased kind, makes his lapses from the straight path to have more powerful effects than is the case with a less advanced man; his retribution and punishment will be equally greater. Inevitably he must pay the price before he is allowed to proceed further upon the Way. As for the group he injures, what should their attitude be? A recognition of the gravity of the error, a wise acceptance of the facts in the case, a refraining from unbrotherly criticism, and a pouring out of love upon the sinning brother:—all this, coupled with such action as will make clear to the onlooking general public that such sins and infringements of the law are not condoned. To this must be added an attitude of mind within the group concerned which will lead them (whilst taking firm action) to help the mistaken brother to see his error, to work out the retributive karma, and then to reinstate him in their regard and respect when due amends have been made.

All people do not develop exactly along the same or parallel lines, and therefore no hard or fast rules can be laid down as to the exact procedure at each initiation, or as to just what centres are to be vivified, or what vision is to be accorded. So much depends upon the ray of the disciple, or his development in any particular direction (people do not usually develop evenly), upon his individual karma, and also upon the exigencies of any special period. This much can be suggested, however: At the first initiation, that of the birth of the Christ, *the heart centre* is the one usually vivified, with the aim in view of the more effective controlling of the astral vehicle, and the rendering of greater service to humanity. After this initiation the initiate is taught principally the facts of the astral plane; he has to stabilise his emotional vehicle and learn to work on the astral plane with the same facility and ease as he does on the physical plane; he is brought in contact with the astral devas; he learns to control the astral elementals; he must function with facility on the lower sub-planes, and the value and quality of his work on the physical plane becomes of increased worth. He passes, at this initiation, out of the Hall of Learning into the Hall of Wisdom. At this time, emphasis is consistently laid on his astral development, although his mental equipment grows steadily.

Many lives may intervene between the first initiation and the second. A long period of many incarnations may elapse before the control of the astral body is perfected, and the initiate is ready for the next step. The analogy is kept in an interesting way in the New Testament in the life of the initiate Jesus. Many years elapsed between the Birth and the Baptism, but the remaining three steps were taken in three years. Once the second initiation is taken the progress will be rapid, the third and fourth following probably in the same life, or the succeeding.

The second initiation forms the *crisis* in the control of the astral body. Just as, at the first initiation, the control of the dense physical has been demonstrated, so here the control of the astral is similarly demonstrated. The sacrifice and death of desire has been the goal of endeavour. Desire itself has been dominated by the Ego, and only that is longed for which is for the good of the whole, and in the line of the will of the Ego, and of the Master. The astral elemental is controlled, the emotional body becomes pure and limpid, and the lower nature is rapidly dying. At this time the Ego grips afresh the two lower vehicles and bends them to his will. The aspiration and longing to serve, love, and progress become so strong that rapid development is usually to be seen. This accounts for the fact that this initiation and the third, frequently (though not invariably) follow each other in one single life. At this period of the world's history such stimulus has been given to evolution that aspiring souls—sensing the dire and crying need of humanity—are sacrificing all in order to meet that need.

Again, we must not make the mistake of thinking that all this follows in the same invariable consecutive steps and stages. Much is done in simultaneous unison, for the labour to control is slow and hard, but in the interim between the first three initiations some definite point in the evolution of each of the three lower vehicles has to be attained and held, before the further expansion of the channel can be safely permitted. Many of us are working on all the three bodies now, as we tread the Probationary Path.

At this initiation, should the ordinary course be followed, (which again is not at all certain) *the throat centre* is vivified. This causes a capacity to turn to account in the Master's service, and for the helping of man, the attainments of the lower mind. It imparts the ability to give forth and utter that which is helpful, possibly in the spoken word, but *surely* in service of some kind.   A vision is accorded of the world's need, and a further portion of the plan shown. The work, then, to be done prior to the taking of the third initiation, is the complete submerging of the personal point of view in the need of the whole. It entails the complete domination of the concrete mind by the Ego.

The succeeding two initiations.

After the second initiation the teaching shifts up a plane. The initiate learns to control his mental vehicle; he develops the capacity to manipulate thought matter, and learns the laws of creative thought building. He functions freely on the four lower sub-planes of the mental plane, and before the third initiation he must,—consciously or unconsciously,—be complete master of the four lower sub-planes in the three planes of the three worlds. His knowledge of the microcosm becomes profound, and he has mastered theoretically and practically, in great measure, the laws of his own nature, hence his ability experimentally to be master on the four lower sub-planes of the physical, astral, and mental planes. The last fact is of interest.   The control of the three higher sub-planes is not yet complete, and here is one of the explanations as to the failures and mistakes of initiates. Their mastery of matter in the three higher sub-planes is not yet perfect; these yet remain to be dominated.

At the third initiation, termed sometimes the Transfiguration, the entire personality is flooded with light from above. It is only after this initiation that the Monad is definitely guiding the Ego, pouring His divine life ever more into the prepared and cleansed channel, just as in the third, or Moon Chain, the Ego individualised the personality through direct contact, a method different to the individualisation as shown in this fourth chain. The law of correspondences, if applied here, might prove very revealing, and might demonstrate an interesting analogy between the methods of individualising in the various chains, and the expansions of consciousness that occur at the different initiations.

Again, a vision is accorded of what lies ahead; the initiate is in a position at all times to recognise the other members of the Great White Lodge, and his psychic faculties are stimulated by the vivification of the *head centres*. It is not necessary nor advisable to develop the synthetic faculties, or clairaudience and clairvoyance, until after this initiation. The aim of all development is the awakening of the spiritual intuition; when this has been done, when the physical body is pure, the astral stable and steady, and the mental body controlled, then the initiate can safely wield and wisely use the psychic faculties for the helping of the race. Not only can he use these faculties, but he is able now to create and vivify thoughtforms that are clear and well-defined, pulsating with the spirit of service and not controlled by lower mind or desire. These thoughtforms will not be (as is the case with those created by the mass of men) disjointed, unconnected, and uncorrelated, but will attain a fair measure of synthesis. Hard and ceaseless must the work be before this can be done, but when the desire nature has been stabilised and purified, then the control of the mind-body comes more easily. Hence the path of the devotee is easier in some ways than that of the intellectual man, for he has learnt the measures of purified desire, and progresses by the requisite stages.

The personality has now reached a point where its vibrations are of a very high order, the matter in all three bodies relatively pure, and its apprehension of the work to be done in the microcosm, and the share to be taken in the work of the macrocosm is very advanced. It is apparent, therefore, why it is only at the third initiation that the great Hierophant, the Lord of the World, Himself officiates. It is the first at which He contacts the initiate. Earlier it would not be possible. For the first two initiations the Hierophant is the Christ, the World-Teacher, the Firstborn among many brethren, one of the earliest of our humanity to take initation. Browning brings out this thought most beautifully in the words found in his poem "Saul":—

> . . . . It shall be
> A face like my face that receives thee; a Man like
> to me,
> Thou shalt love and be loved by, forever;
> A Hand like this hand
> Shall throw open the gates of new life to thee!
> See the Christ stand!

But when the initiate has made still further progress, and has taken two initiations, a change comes. The Lord of the World, the Ancient of Days, the ineffable Ruler Himself administers the third initiation. Why has this become possible? Because now the fully consecrated physical body can safely bear the vibrations of the two other bodies when they return to its shelter from the Presence of the KING; because now the purified astral and controlled mental can safely stand before that KING. When purified and controlled they *stand* and for the first time *consciously* vibrate to the Ray of the Monad, then with prepared bodies can the ability to see and hear on all the planes be granted and achieved, and the faculty of reading and comprehending the records be safely employed, for with fuller knowledge comes added power. The heart is now sufficiently pure and loving, and the intellect sufficiently stable to stand the strain of *knowing*.

Before the fourth initiation can be taken, the work of

training is intensified, and the hastening and accumulation of knowledge has to be unbelievably rapid. The initiate has frequent access to the library of occult books, and after this initiation he can contact not only the Master with Whom he is linked and with Whom he has worked consciously for a long time, but he can contact and assist (in measure) the Chohans, the Bodhisattva, and the Manu.

He has also to grasp the laws of the three lower planes intellectually, and likewise wield them for the aiding of the scheme of evolution. He studies the cosmic plans and has to master the charts; he becomes versed in occult technicalities and develops fourth dimensional vision, if he has not already done so. He learns to direct the activities of the building devas, and at the same time, he works continually at the development of his spiritual nature. He begins rapidly to co-ordinate the buddhic vehicle, and in its co-ordination he develops the power of synthesis, at first in small measure, and gradually in fuller detail.

By the time the fourth initiation is taken the initiate has mastered perfectly the fifth sub-plane, and is therefore adept,—to use a technical phrase,—on the five lower subplanes of the physical, astral, and mental planes, and is well on the way to master the sixth. His buddhic vehicle can function on the two lower sub-planes of the buddhic plane.

The life of the man who takes the fourth initiation, or the Crucifixion, is usually one of great sacrifice and suffering. It is the life of the man who makes the Great Renunciation, and even exoterically it is seen to be strenuous, hard, and painful. He has laid all, even his perfected personality, upon the altar of sacrifice, and stands bereft of all. All is renounced, friends, money, reputation, character, standing in the world, family, and even life itself.

The final initiations.

After the fourth initiation not much remains to be done. The domination of the sixth sub-plane goes forward with rapidity, and the matter of the higher sub-planes of the buddhic is co-ordinated. The initiate is admitted into closer fellowship in the Lodge, and his contact with the devas is more complete. He is rapidly exhausting the resources of the Hall of Wisdom, and is mastering the most intricate plans and charts. He becomes adept in the significance of colour and sound, can wield the law in the three worlds, and can contact his Monad with more freedom than the majority of the human race can contact their Egos. He is in charge, also, of large work, teaching many pupils, aiding in many schemes, and is gathering under him those who are to assist him in future times. This refers only to those who stay to help humanity on this globe; we will deal later with some of the lines of work that stretch before the Adept if He passes away from earth service.

After the fifth initiation the man is perfected as far as this scheme goes, though he may, if he will, take two further initiations.

To achieve the sixth initiation the Adept has to take a very intensive course in planetary occultism. A Master wields the law in the three worlds, whilst a Chohan of the sixth initiation wields the law in the chain on all levels; a Chohan of the seventh initiation wields the law in the solar system.

It will be apparent that, should he search these subjects with application, the student will find much that concerns him personally, even though the ceremony itself may be far ahead. By the study of the process and the purpose he may become aware of the great fundamental fact that the method of initiation is the method of:—

a. Force realisation.
b. Force application.
c. Force utilisation.

The initiate of every degree, from the humble initiate of the first degree, making for the first time his contact with a certain type of specialised force, up to the emancipated buddha of the seventh degree, is dealing with energy of some kind or other. The stages of development of the aspirant might be expressed as follows:—

1. He has to become aware, through discrimination, of the energy or force of his own lower self.
2. He has to impose upon that energetic rhythm one that is higher, until that lower rhythm is superseded by the higher, and the old method of expressing energy dies out entirely.
3. He then is permitted, by gradually expanding realisations, to contact and—under guidance—to employ certain forms of group energy, until the time comes when he is in a position scientifically to wield planetary force. The length of time taken over his final stage is entirely dependent upon the progress he makes in the service of his race and in the development of those powers of the soul which are the natural sequence of spiritual unfoldment.

The application of the Rod of Initiation at the first two initiations by the Bodhisattva enables the initiate to control and utilise the force of the lower self, the true sanctified energy of the personality in service; at the third initiation the application of the Rod by the One Initiator makes available in a vastly more extensive manner the force of the higher self or Ego, and brings into play on the physical plane the entire energy stored up during numerous incarnations in the causal vehicle. At the fourth initiation the energy of his egoic group becomes his to use for the good of planetary evolution, and at the fifth initiation the force or energy of the planet (esoterically understood, and not merely the force or energy of the material globe) is at his disposal. During these five initiations those two great beings, the Bodhisattva first, and then the One Initiator, the Lord of the World, Sanat Kumara, are the administrators or hierophants. After these ceremonies, should the initiate choose to take the two final initiations which it is possible to take in this solar system, a still higher type of energy in expression of the One Self comes into play, and can only be hinted at. At the seventh initiation that One of Whom Sanat Kumara is the manifestation, the Logos of our scheme on His own plane, becomes the Hierophant. At the sixth initiation the expression of this Existence on an intermediate plane, a Being Who must at present remain nameless, wields the Rod and administers the oath and secret. In these three expressions of hierarchical government—Sanat Kumara on the periphery of the three worlds, the Nameless One on the confines of the high planes of human evolution, and the planetary Spirit himself at the final stage—we have the three great manifestations of the Planetary Logos Himself. Through the Planetary Logos at the final great initiation flows the power of the Solar Logos, and He it is Who reveals to the initiate that the Absolute is consciousness in its fullest expression, though at the stage of human existence the Absolute must be regarded as unconsciousness.

Each of the great initiations is but the synthesis of the smaller ones, and only as man seeks ever to expand his consciousness in the affairs of daily life can he expect to achieve those later stages which are but culminations of the many earlier. Students must get rid of the idea that if they are "very good and altruistic" suddenly some day they will stand before the Great Lord. They are putting effect before cause. Goodness and altruism grow out of realisation and service, and holiness of character is the outcome of those expansions of consciousness which a man brings about within himself through strenuous effort and endeavour. Therefore it is here and now that man can prepare himself for initiation, and this he does, not by dwelling upon the ceremonial aspect, as so many do in excited anticipation, but by working systematically and enduringly at the steady development of the mental body, by the strenuous and arduous process of controlling the astral body so that it becomes responsive to three vibrations:—

    a. That from the Ego.
    b. That from the Master.
    c. Those from his brothers everywhere around him. He becomes *sensitive* to the voice of his higher self, thus working off karma under the intelligent guidance of his own Ego. He becomes conscious, via the Ego, of the vibration emanating from his Master; he learns to *feel* it ever more and more, and to respond to it ever more fully; finally, he becomes increasingly sensitive to the joys and pains and sorrows of those he daily contacts; he feels them to be his joys and pains and sorrows, and yet he is not incapacitated thereby.

CHAPTER X

THE UNIVERSALITY OF INITIATION

It has been emphasised many times in the occult teachings that the process of initiation, as it is usually understood, is an abnormal and not a normal one. All progression in the realm of consciousness is naturally by a graded series of awakenings, but this would proceed much more gradually and cover a longer period of time than is the case under our present planetary conditions. This particular mode of developing the consciousness of the human family was initiated by the Hierarchy during the Atlantean root-race at the latter end of the fourth sub-race, and will persist until the middle of the next round. At that time the needed stimulus will have been imparted, and as three-fifths of the human family will then have esoterically "set their feet upon the path," and a large percentage of them will then be in process of becoming the Path itself, the more normal routine will again be resumed.

Initiation on the various planets.

The process of stimulation of the human Egos by means of graded instructions, and the application of the dynamic electrical force of the Rod is employed on three of the planets of our system at this time. It is instituted during every fourth round, and its peculiar interest lies in the fact that the emphasis for the fourth Creative Hierarchy in every fourth chain and globe during the fourth round is laid upon the fourth initiation, that of the Crucifixion. The fourth Creative Hierarchy is the great expression of the conscious will and sacrifice of the Solar Logos, and the great symbol of the intelligent union of spirit and matter. Hence the fourth initiation, with its presentation of these cosmic truths, and its epitomising of the purpose of this fundamental sacrifice, has a pre-eminent place.

The student needs to remind himself that the other planetary schemes, though fundamentally the same as our fourth scheme, yet have their profound differences in manifestation, due to the varying characteristics and the individual karma of the incarnating Planetary Logos or Ray. These differences affect:—

a. The initiatory process, both in its ceremonial and altruistic aspects.

b. The application of the Rod, for the type of force which it embodies, when brought into conjunction with the differentiated force of the planetary type, produces results of varying nature and degree.

c. The seasons of initiation. The Egos in incarnation on any planet will—according to ray type—be easily stimulated or not as the case may be, according to astrological conditions, and this will produce shorter or more protracted periods of development prior to or between each initiation.

d. The electrical phenomena produced on the higher planes, as more and more the human units esoterically "blaze forth." It must be remembered that the entire solar system, with all that is included therein, is expressing itself in terms of *light,* and that the process of initiation might therefore be regarded as one in which the different points of light (or human sparks) are stimulated, their radiance and temperature increased, and the sphere of influence of each light extended in radius.

The three planetary schemes wherein the great experiment of initiation is being tried are the Earth, Venus, and one other. Venus was the first sphere of experiment, and the success of the endeavour and the force generated was the cause of a similar effort being made on our planet. No planet increases its store of force, and consequently its sphere of influence, without incurring obligations and affecting other schemes; the interchange of force and energy between these two planets, Earth and Venus, is continuous. A similar process has but lately been instituted on another planetary scheme, and when, in the next round, our Earth attains a point in evolution analogous to that of the Venusian scheme at the time its influence was felt by us, then we shall aid in the stimulation of still another group of planetary Egos; we shall assist in the institution of a similar procedure among the sons of men in another scheme.

In the three great planetary schemes, Neptune, Uranus, and Saturn, the method of initiation will not be employed. They will be the recipients of those who are esoterically "saved" from among the other schemes. That is to say that all those who, in any scheme, achieve the needed expansions of consciousness (such as will be achieved by the majority of the human family prior to the middle of the next great cycle, or round), will be considered "saved," whilst the remainder will be held to be failures, and will be held over for further development during later periods, or will be transferred to those planetary schemes which from the point of view of time are not so far advanced as our Earth scheme. These three major schemes are the absorbers and synthesisers of the energy of the others.

Initiation and the Devas.

The question may be asked whether the devas undergo initiation, and we might deal briefly with the point here.

Initiation has to do with the conscious development of the self, and concerns the wisdom aspect of the One Self. It presupposes the development of the intelligence principle, and involves the apprehension by the human unit of purpose and of will, and his intelligent participation therein through love and service. The devas, with the exception of those greater devas who have in earlier cycles passed through the human kingdom and are now co-operating in the evolution of man, are not as yet self-conscious. They grow and develop through *feeling* and not through the power of conscious thought. Man, however, grows through expansions of self-conscious realisation, self-initiated and self-imposed. It is the line of aspiration and of conscious endeavour, and is the most difficult line of development in the solar system, for it follows not along the line of least resistance, but seeks to initiate and impose a higher rhythm. The devas follow the line of least resistance, and seek to appropriate and experience in fullest tide of feeling and sentiency the vibration of *things as they are*. Therefore the method for them is an ever-increasing intensity of appreciation for the feeling of the moment, and not, as in man, an ever-increasing depreciation of things as they are, or of the material aspect, which leads to an endeavour to reach out and enfold within his consciousness the subjective reality, or the things of the spirit—this in contradistinction to the objective unreality, or the things of matter. The devas seek to feel, whilst man seeks to know. For the former, then, those expansions of consciousness which we call Initiation, exist not, except in the cases of those advanced beings who, having passed through the human stage, both feel and know, and who, under the evolutionary law, expand their knowledge in ever-increasing degree.

Cosmic influences and solar initiations.

All that can be done here in dealing with this profound subject is to enumerate briefly some of the cosmic influences which definitely affect our earth, and produce results in the consciousness of men everywhere, and which, during the process of initiation, bring about certain specific phenomena.

First and foremost is the energy or force emanating from the *sun Sirius*. If it might be so expressed, the energy of thought, or mind force, in its totality, reaches the solar system from a distant cosmic centre via Sirius. Sirius acts as the transmitter, or the focalising centre, whence emanate those influences which produce self-consciousness in man. During initiation, by means of the Rod of Initiation (acting as a subsidiary transmitter and as a powerful magnet) this energy is momentarily intensified, and applied to the centres of the initiate with terrific force; were it not that the Hierophant and the two sponsors of the initiate pass it primarily through their bodies, it would be more than he could stand. This increase of mind energy results in an expansion and an apprehension of the truth as it is, and is lasting in its effects. It is felt primarily in the throat centre, the great organ of creation through sound.

Another type of energy reaches man from the *Pleiades,* passing through the Venusian scheme to us, just as the Sirian energy passes through the Saturnian. It has a definite effect upon the causal body, and serves to stimulate the heart centre.

A third type of energy is applied to the initiate, and affects his head centre. It emanates from that one of the seven stars of the *Great Bear* whose ensouling life holds the same relationship to our Planetary Logos as the Ego does to a human being. This energy, therefore, is seven-fold, and differs according to a man's ray or type.

It is not possible here to state the order of the application of these varying types of energy, nor to give the initiation during which the man contacts the different types. These facts involve the secrets of the mysteries, and no purpose is served by revealing them. Other types of force from certain of the planetary schemes, as well as from cosmic centres, are brought into play by the Initiator and transmitted through the medium of the Rod to the various centres in the initiate's three vehicles, the mental, the astral, and the etheric centres. At the fourth initiation a specialised type of force from a centre which must remain nameless is applied to a man's causal body, and is one of the causes of its final disintegration.

In thinking of this matter of the attainment of the sons of men, we must recognise that as mankind completes one unification after another, the "Heavenly Men" on intuitional levels and on spiritual levels are completed, and in their turn go to the formation of the centres in the great "Heavenly Men" of the solar system. These seven Heavenly Men, in Whose bodies each human Monad and each deva finds his place, form the seven centres in the body of the Logos. He, in His turn, forms the Heart centre (for God is Love) of a still greater Entity. The consummation of all for this solar system will be when the Logos takes His fifth initiation. When all the sons of men attain the fifth initiation, He achieves. This is a great mystery and incomprehensible to us.

CHAPTER XI

THE PARTICIPANTS IN THE MYSTERIES

The participants in the mysteries are generally known, and no secret has been made of the general personnel and procedure. It is only sought here to impart a greater sense of reality to the data already given by a fuller exposition and a more pointed reference to the parts played by such during the ceremony. At this stage the student would be wise to bear in mind certain things as he ponders upon the mysteries touched upon here:—

That care must be taken to interpret all here given in terms of spirit and not of matter or form. We are dealing entirely with the subjective or consciousness aspect of manifestation, and with that which lies back of the objective form. This realisation will save the student from much later confusion.

That we are considering facts which are substantial and real on the *mental plane*—the plane on which all the major initiations take place—but which are not materialised on the physical plane, and are not physical plane phenomena. The link between the two planes exists in the continuity of consciousness which the initiate will have developed, and which will enable him to bring through to the physical brain, occurrences and happenings upon the subjective planes of life.

Corroboration of these occurrences, and proof of the accuracy of the transmitted knowledge will demonstrate as follows:—

In and through the etheric centres. These centres will be greatly stimulated, and will, through their increased in-herent energy, enable the initiate to accomplish more in the path of service than he ever before dreamed possible. His dreams and ideals become, not possibilities, but demonstrating facts in manifestation.

The physical centres, such as the pineal gland and the pituitary body, will begin to develop rapidly, and he will become conscious of the awakening of the "siddhis," or powers of the soul, in the higher connotation of the words. He will be aware of the process of conscious control, and of the self-initiated manipulations of the above powers. He will realise the methods of egoic contact and the right direction of force.

The nervous system, through which the emotional body or astral nature works, will become highly sensitised, yet strong withal. The brain will become ever more rapidly an acute transmitter of the inner impulses. This fact is of real importance, and will bring about—as its significance becomes more apparent— a revolution in the attitude of educators, of physicians and others, to the development of the nervous system and the healing of nervous disorders.

Occult memory. The initiate finally becomes aware in-creasingly of the growth of that inner recollection, or "oc-cult memory," which concerns the work of the Hierarchy and primarily his share in the general plan. When the initiate, who occultly recalls, in his waking consciousness, a ceremonial fact, finds all these manifestations of increased growth and conscious realisation *in himself,* then the truth of his inner assurance is proven and substantiated to him.

It must be remembered that this inner substantiation is of no value to anyone but the initiate. He has to prove himself to the outer world through his life of service and the work accomplished, and thereby call forth from all his environing associates a recognition that will show itself in a sanctified emulation and a strenuous effort to tread the same path, actuated ever by the same motive,—that of service and brotherhood, not self-aggrandisement and selfish acquirement. It should also be remembered that if the above is true in connection with the work, it is still more true in connection with the initiate himself. *Initiation is a strictly personal matter with a universal application*. It rests upon his inner attainment. The initiate will know for himself when the event occurs and needs no one to tell him of it. The expansion of consciousness called initiation must include the physical brain or it is of no value. As those lesser expansions of consciousness which we undergo normally every day, and call "learning" something or other, have reference to the apprehension by the physical brain of an imparted fact or apprehended circumstance, so with the greater expansions which are the outcome of the many lesser.

At the same time, it is quite possible for men to be functioning on the physical plane and to be actively employed in world service who have no recollection of having undergone the initiatory process, yet who, nevertheless, may have taken the first or second initiation in a previous or earlier life. This is the result, simply, of a lack of "bridging" from one life to another, or it may be the outcome of a definite decision by the Ego. A man may be able better to work off certain karma and to carry out certain work for the Lodge if he is free from occult occupation and mystic introspection during the period of any one earth life. There are many such amongst the sons of men at this time who have previously taken the first initiation, and a few who have taken the second, but who are nevertheless quite unaware of it, yet their centres and nervous organisation carry proof to those who have the inner vision. If initiation is taken for the first time in any life, the recollection of it extends to the physical brain.

Curiosity, or even ordinary good living, never brought a man to the Portal of Initiation. Curiosity, by arousing a strong vibration in a man's lower nature, only serves to swing him away from, instead of towards the goal he is interested in; whilst ordinary good living, when not furthered by a life of utter sacrifice for others, and by a reticence, humility, and disinterestedness of a very unusual kind, may serve to build good vehicles which will be of use in another incarnation, but will not serve to break down those barriers, outer and inner, and overcome those opposing forces and energies which stand between a "good" man and the ceremony of initiation.

The Path of Discipleship is a difficult one to tread, and the Path of Initiation harder still; an initiate is but a battle-scarred warrior, the victor in many a hard-won fight; he speaks not of his achievements, for he is too busy with the great work in hand; he makes no reference to himself or to all that he has accomplished, save to deprecate the littleness of what has been done. Nevertheless, to the world he is ever a man of large influence, the wielder of spiritual power, the embodier of ideals, the worker for humanity, who unfailingly brings results which succeeding generations will recognise. He is one who, in spite of all this great achievement, is seldom understood by his own generation. He is frequently the butt of men's tongues, and frequently all that he does is misinterpreted; he lays his all—time, money, influence, reputation, and all that the world considers worth while—upon the altar of altruistic service, and frequently offers his life as a final gift, only to find that those whom he has served throw his gift back to him, scorn his renunciation, and label him with unsavory names. But the initiate cares not, for his is the privilege to see somewhat into the future, and therefore he realises that the force he has generated will in due course of time bring to fulfilment the plan; he knows also that his name and effort are noted in the archives of the Lodge, and that the "Silent Watcher" over the affairs of men has taken notice.

Planetary Existences.

In considering now the personalities taking part in the initiation ceremonies, the first to be dealt with are Those Who are termed Planetary Existences. This refers to those great Beings who, for a period of planetary manifestation, overshadow or stay with our humanity. They are not very many in number, for the majority of the Great Ones pass on steadily and increasingly to other and higher work, as Their places can be taken and Their functions carried on by members of our earth evolution, both deva and human.

Among Those directly connected with our Lodge of Masters in its various divisions upon the planet, the following might be enumerated:—

The *"Silent Watcher,"* that great Entity Who is the informing life of the planet, and Who holds the same position to the Lord of the World, Sanat Kumara, as the Ego does to the lower self of man. Some idea of the high stage of evolution of this Great Being may be gathered from the analogous degree of evolutionary difference existing between a human being and a perfected adept. From the standpoint of our planetary scheme, this great Life has no greater, and He is, as far as we are concerned, a correspondence to the personal God of the Christian. He works through His representative on the physical plane, Sanat Kumara, Who is the focal point for His life and energy. He holds the world within His aura. This great Existence is only contacted directly by the adept who has taken the fifth initiation, and is proceeding to take the other two, the sixth and seventh. Once a year, at the Wesak Festival, the Lord Buddha, sanctioned by the Lord of the World, carries to the assembled humanity a dual stream of force, that emanating from the Silent Watcher, supplemented by the more focalised energy of the Lord of the World. This dual energy He pours out in blessing over the people gathered at the ceremony in the Himalayas, and from them in turn it flows out to all peoples and tongues and races. It may not perhaps be generally known that at a certain crisis during the Great War the Hierarchy of our planet deemed it well nigh necessary to invoke the aid of the Silent Watcher, and—employing the great mantram whereby the Buddha can be reached—called the attention of the latter, and sought his agency with the Planetary Logos. In consultation between the Planetary Logos, the Lord of the World, one of the Buddhas of Activity, the Buddha, the Mahachohan, and the Manu (these names are given in order of their relative evolutionary stage) it was decided to watch proceedings a little longer before interfering with the trend of affairs, as the karma of the planet would have been delayed should the strife have been ended too soon. Their confidence in the ability of men duly to adjust conditions was justified, and interference proved needless. This conference took place at Shamballa. This is mentioned to show the close scrutiny given to everything concerning the affairs of men by the various Planetary Existences. It is literally true, in an occult sense, that "not a sparrow falleth" without its fall being noticed.

It may be asked why the Bodhisattva was not included in the conference. The reason was that the war was in the department of the Manu, and members of the Hierarchy concern Themselves with that which is strictly Their own business; the Mahachohan, being the embodiment of the

intelligent or manasic principle, participates in all conferences. In the next great strife the department of religions
will be involved, and the Bodhisattva intimately concerned.
His Brother, the Manu, will then be relatively exempt, and
will proceed with His own affairs. And yet withal there is
the closest co-operation in all departments, with no loss of
energy. Owing to the unity of consciousness of those who
are free from the three lower planes, what transpires in one
department is known in the others.

As the Planetary Logos is only concerned in the two
final initiations, which are not compulsory as are the earlier
five, it serves no purpose to enlarge upon His work. These
initiations are taken upon the buddhic and atmic planes,
whereas the first five are taken upon the mental.

The Lord of the World, the One Initiator, He Who is
called in the Bible "The Ancient of Days," and in the Hindu
Scriptures the First Kumara, He, Sanat Kumara it is, Who
from His throne at Shamballa in the Gobi desert, presides
over the Lodge of Masters, and holds in His hands the
reins of government in all the three departments. Called
in some Scriptures "the Great Sacrifice," He has chosen
to watch over the evolution of men and devas until all have
been occultly "saved." He it is Who decides upon the
"advancements" in the different departments, and Who
settles who shall fill the vacant posts; He it is Who, four
times a year, meets in conference with all the Chohans
and Masters, and authorises what shall be done to further
the ends of evolution.

Occasionally, too, He meets with initiates of lesser degree, but only at times of great crises, when some individual is given the opportunity to bring peace out of strife,
and to kindle a blaze whereby rapidly crystallising forms
are destroyed and the imprisoned life consequently set free.

At stated periods in the year the Lodge meets, and at

the Wesak Festival gathers under His jurisdiction for three purposes:

1. To contact planetary force through the medium of the Buddha.
2. To hold the principal of the quarterly conferences.
3. To admit to the ceremony of initiation those who are ready in all grades.

Three other initiation ceremonies take place during the year:—

1. For the minor initiations administered by the Bodhisattva, all of which are in the department of the Mahachohan, and on one or other of the four lesser rays, the rays of attribute.
2. For the major initiations on one or other of the three major rays, the rays of aspect, which are administered by the Bodhisattva, and are therefore the first two initiations.
3. For the higher three initiations at which Sanat Kumara wields the Rod.

At all initiations the Lord of the World is present, but at the first two He holds a position similar to that held by the Silent Watcher, when Sanat Kumara administers the oath at the third, fourth and fifth initiations. His power streams forth and the flashing forth of the star before the initiate is the signal of His approval, but the initiate does not see Him face to face until the third initiation.

The function of the *three Kumaras,* or the three Buddhas of Activity at initiation is interesting. They are three aspects of the one aspect, and the pupils of Sanat Kumara. Though Their functions are many and varied, and concern primarily the forces and energies of nature, and the direction of the building agencies, They have a vital connection with the applicant for initiation, inasmuch as They each embody the force or energy of one or other of the three higher subplanes of the mental plane. Therefore at the third initiation one of these Kumaras transmits to the causal body of the initiate that energy which destroys third subplane matter, and thus brings about part of the destruction of the vehicle; at the fourth initiation another Buddha transmits second plane force, and at the fifth, first subplane force is similarly passed into the remaining atoms of the causal vehicle, producing the final liberation. The work done by the second Kumara, with second subplane force, is in this solar system the most important in connection with the egoic body, and produces its complete dissipation, whereas the final application causes the atoms themselves (which formed that body) to disperse.

During the initiation ceremony, when the initiate stands before the Lord of the World, these three great Beings form a triangle, within whose lines of force the initiate finds himself. At the first two initiations, wherein the Bodhisattva functions as the Hierophant, the Mahachohan, the Manu, and a Chohan who temporarily represents the second department perform a similar office. At the highest two initiations, those three Kumaras who are called "the esoteric Kumaras" form a triangle wherein the initiate stands, when he faces the Planetary Logos.

These facts are imparted to teach two things, first, the unity of the method, second, that the truism "as above so below" is an occult fact in nature.

At the final two initiations many members of the Hierarchy who are, if one might so express it, extra-planetary, and who function outside the dense physical and the etheric globe of our planet, take part, but a stricter enumeration is needless. Sanat Kumara is still the Hierophant, yet in a very esoteric manner it is the Planetary Logos Himself who officiates. They are merged at that time into one Identity, manifesting different aspects.

Suffice it to say, in concluding this brief statement, that the making of an initiate is an affair with a dual effect, for it involves ever a passing on of some adept or initiate to a higher grade or to other work, and the coming in under the Law of some human being who is in process of attainment. Therefore it is a thing of great moment, involving group activity, group loyalty, and united endeavour, and much may depend upon the wisdom of admitting a man to high office and to a place in the council chambers of the Hierarchy.

The Departmental Heads.

> The Manu.
> The Bodhisattva.
> The Mahachohan.

As has been said, these three great Beings, represent the triplicity of all manifestation, and might be expressed under the following form, remembering that all this deals with subjectivity, and therefore with the evolution of consciousness and primarily with self-consciousness in man.

Consciousness

The Manu	*The Bodhisattva*	*The Mahachohan*
Matter aspect	Spirit aspect	Intelligence aspect.
Form	Life	Mind.
The Not-Self	The Self	The relation between.
Body	Spirit	Soul.

Or, in words strictly dealing with self-conscious realisation.

Politics	Religion	Science.
Government	Beliefs	Civilisation.
Races	Faiths	Education.

All human beings belong to one or other of these three departments, and all are of equal importance, for Spirit and matter are one. All are so interdependent, being but expressions of one life, that the endeavour to express the functions of the three departments in tabular form is liable to lead to error.

The three Great Lords closely co-operate in the work, for that work is one, just as man, though a triplicity, is yet an individual unit. The human being is a form through which a spiritual life or entity is manifesting, and employing the intelligence under evolutionary law.

Therefore the Great Lords are closely connected with the initiations of a human unit. They are too occupied with greater affairs and with group activities to have any relationship with a man until he stands upon the probationary path. When he has, through his own effort, brought himself on to the Path of Discipleship, the particular Master Who has him under supervision reports to the Head of one of the three departments (this being dependent upon a man's ray) that he is nearing the Portal of Initiation and should be ready for the great step during such and such a life. Each life, and later each year, report is made, until the final year upon the Path of Probation, when closer and more frequent reports are handed in. During this final year also, the applicant's name is submitted to the Lodge, and after his own Master has reported upon him, and his record has been briefly summarised, his name is balloted, and sponsors are arranged.

During the initiation ceremony the important factors are:—

1. The Initiator.
2. The triangle of force formed by three adepts or three Kumaras.
3. The sponsors.

In the case of the first two initiations, two Masters stand, one on each side of the applicant, within the triangle; at the third, fourth and fifth initiations, the Mahachohan and the Bodhisattva perform the function of sponsor; at the sixth and seventh initiations two great Beings, Who must remain nameless, stand within the esoteric triangle. The work of the sponsors is to pass through Their bodies the force or electrical energy emanating from the Rod of Initiation. This force, through radiation, circles around the triangle and is supplemented by the force of the three guardians; it next passes through the centres of the sponsors, being transmitted by an act of will to the initiate.

Enough has been said elsewhere in this book anent the Lodge of Masters and Their relation to the applicant for initiation, whilst the work of the initiate himself has been likewise touched upon. That work is not unknown to the children of men everywhere, but remains as yet an ideal and a far-off possibility. Yet when a man strives to reach that ideal, to make it a demonstrating fact within himself, he will find that it becomes not only a possibility, but something attainable, provided he strives sufficiently. The first initiation is within the reach of many, but the necessary one-pointedness and the firm belief in the reality ahead, coupled to a willingness to sacrifice all rather than turn back, are deterrents to the many. If this book serves no other purpose than to spur some one to renewed believing effort, it will not have been written in vain.

CHAPTER XII

THE TWO REVELATIONS

We can now consider the stages of the initiation ceremony, which are five in number, as follows:—

1. The "Presence" revealed.
2. The "Vision" seen.
3. The application of the Rod, affecting:—

    a. The bodies.
    b. The centres.
    c. The causal vehicle.

4. The administration of the oath.
5. The giving of the "Secret" and the Word.

These points are given in due order, and it must be remembered that this order is not idly arranged, but carries the
initiate on from revelation to revelation until the culmi-
nating stage wherein is committed to him one of the secrets
and one of the five words of power which open to him
the various planes, with all their evolutions. All that is
aimed at here is to indicate the five main divisions into
which the initiation ceremony naturally divides itself, and
the student must bear in mind that each of these five stages
is in itself a complete ceremony, and capable of detailed division.

Let us now take up the various points, dwelling briefly
upon each, and remembering that words but limit and confine the true meaning.

The revelation of the "Presence."

Right through the later periods of the cycle of incarnation wherein the man is juggling with the pairs of opposites, and through discrimination is becoming aware of reality and unreality, there is growing up in his mind a realisation that he himself is an immortal Existence, an eternal God, and a portion of Infinity. Ever the link between the man on the physical plane and this inner Ruler becomes clearer until the great revelation is made. Then comes a moment in his existence when the man stands consciously face to face with his real Self and knows himself to be that Self in reality and not just theoretically; he becomes aware of the God within, not through the sense of hearing, or through attention to the inner voice directing and controlling, and called the "voice of conscience." This time the recognition is through *sight and direct vision*. He now responds not only to that which is heard, but also to that which he sees.

It is known that the first senses developed in a child are hearing, touch, and sight; the infant becomes aware of sound and turns his head; he feels and touches; finally, he consciously sees, and in these three senses the personality is co-ordinated. These are the three vital senses. Taste and smell follow later, but life can be lived without them, and should they be absent, the man remains practically unhandicapped in his contacts on the physical plane. On the path of inner, or subjective development, the sequence is the same.

Hearing—response to the voice of conscience, as it guides, directs, and controls. This covers the period of strictly normal evolution.

Touch—response to control or vibration, and the recognition of that which lies outside of the separated human unit on the physical plane. This covers the period of gradual spiritual unfoldment, the Paths of Probation and of Discipleship right up to the door of initiation. The man touches at intervals that which is higher than himself; he becomes aware of the "touch" of the Master, of the egoic vibration and of group vibration, and through this occult sense of touch he accustoms himself to that which is inner and subtle. He reaches out after that which concerns the higher self, and through touching unseen things, habituates himself to them.

Finally, *Sight*—that inner vision which is produced through the initiation process, yet which is withal but the recognition of faculty, always present yet unknown. Just as an infant has eyes which are perfectly good and clear from birth, yet there comes a day wherein the conscious recognition of that which is seen is first to be noted, so with the human unit undergoing spiritual unfoldment. The medium of the inner sight has ever existed, and that which can be seen is always present, but the recognition of the majority as yet exists not.

This "recognition" by the initiate is the first great step in the initiation ceremony, and until it has transpired all the other stages must wait. That which is recognised differs at the different initiations, and might be roughly summarised as follows:—

The Ego, the reflection of the Monad, is in itself a triplicity, as is all else in nature, and reflects the three aspects of divinity, just as the Monad reflects on a higher plane the three aspects—will, love-wisdom, and active intelligence—of the Deity. Therefore:

At the first initiation the initiate becomes aware of the third, or lowest, aspect of the Ego, that of active intelligence. He is brought face to face with that manifestation of the great solar angel (Pitri) who is himself, the real self. He knows now past all disturbance that that manifestation of intelligence is that eternal Entity who has for ages past been demonstrating its powers on the physical plane through his successive incarnations.

At the second initiation this great Presence is seen as a duality, and another aspect shines forth before him. He becomes aware that this radiant Life, Who is identified with himself, is not only intelligence in action but also is love-wisdom in origin. He merges his consciousness with this Life, and becomes one with it so that on the physical plane, through the medium of that personal self, that Life is seen as intelligent love expressing itself.

At the third initiation the Ego stands before the initiate as a perfected triplicity. Not only is the Self known to be intelligent, active love, but it is revealed also as a fundamental will or purpose, with which the man immediately identifies himself, and knows that the three worlds hold for him in the future naught, but only serve as a sphere for active service, wrought out in love towards the accomplishment of a purpose which has been hid during the ages in the heart of the Self. That purpose, being now revealed, can be intelligently co-operated with, and thus matured.

These profound revelations shine forth before the initiate in a triple manner:—

As a radiant angelic existence. This is seen by the inner eye with the same accuracy of vision and judgment as when a man stands face to face with another member of the human family. The great solar Angel, Who embodies the real man and is his expression on the plane of higher mind, is literally his divine ancestor, the "Watcher" Who, through long cycles of incarnation, has poured Himself out in sacrifice in order that man might BE.

As a sphere of radiant fire, linked with the initiate standing before it by that magnetic thread of fire which passes through all his bodies and terminates within the centre of the physical brain. This "silver thread" (as it is rather inaccurately called in the Bible, where the description of its loosing of the physical body and subsequent withdrawal is found) emanates from the heart centre of the solar Angel, linking thus heart and brain,—that great duality manifesting in this solar system, love and intelligence. This fiery sphere is linked likewise with many others belonging to the same group and ray, and thus it is a literal fact in demonstration that on the higher planes we are all one. One life pulsates and circulates through all, via the fiery strands. This is part of the revelation which comes to a man who stands in the "Presence" with his eyes occultly opened.

As a many tinted Lotus of nine petals. These petals are arranged in three circles around a central set of three closely folded petals, which shield what is called in the eastern books "The Jewel in the Lotus." This Lotus is a thing of rare beauty, pulsating with life and radiant with all the colours of the rainbow, and at the first three initiations the three circles are revealed in order, until at the fourth initiation the initiate stands before a still greater revelation, and learns the secret of that which lies within the central bud. In this connection the third initiation differs somewhat from the other two, inasmuch as through the power of a still more exalted Hierophant than the Bodhisattva, the electrical fire of pure Spirit, latent in the heart of the Lotus, is first contacted.

In all these words, "solar angel," "sphere of fire," and "lotus," lies hid some aspect of the central mystery of human life, but it will only be apparent to those who have eyes to see. The mystic significance of these pictorial phrases will prove only a snare or a basis for incredulity to the man who seeks to materialise them unduly. The thought of an immortal existence, of a divine Entity, of a great centre of fiery energy, and of the full flower of evolution, lies hidden in these terms, and they must be thus considered.

At the fourth initiation, the initiate is brought into the Presence of that aspect of Himself which is called "His Father in Heaven." He is brought face to face with his own Monad, that pure spiritual essence on the highest plane but one, which is to his Ego or higher self what that Ego is to the personality or lower self.

This Monad has expressed itself on the mental plane through the Ego in a triple fashion, but now all aspects of the mind, as we understand it, are lacking. The solar angel hitherto contacted has withdrawn himself, and the form through which he functioned (the egoic or causal body) has gone, and naught is left but love-wisdom and that dynamic will which is the prime characteristic of Spirit. The lower self has served the purposes of the Ego, and has been discarded; the Ego likewise has served the purposes of the Monad, and is no longer required, and the initiate stands free of both, fully liberated and able to contact the Monad, as earlier he learned to contact the Ego. For the remainder of his appearances in the three worlds he is governed only by will and purpose, self-initiated, and creates his body of manifestation, and thus controls (within karmic limits) his own times and seasons. The karma here referred to is planetary karma, and not personal.

At this fourth initiation he contacts the love aspect of the Monad, and at the fifth the will aspect, and thus completes his contacts, responds to all necessary vibrations, and is master on the five planes of human evolution.

Further, it is at the third, the fourth, and the fifth initiations that he becomes aware also of that "Presence" which enfolds even that spiritual Entity, his own Monad.

He sees his Monad as one with the Planetary Logos. Through the channel of his own Monad he sees the self-same aspects (which that Monad embodies) on a wider scale, and the Planetary Logos, Who ensouls all the Monads on His ray, is thus revealed. This truth is well-nigh impossible to express in words, and concerns the relation of the electrical point of fire, which is the Monad, to the five-pointed star, which reveals the Presence of the Planetary Logos to the initiate. This is practically incomprehensible to the average man for whom this book is written.

At the sixth initiation, the initiate, functioning consciously as the love-aspect of the Monad, is brought (via his "Father") into a still vaster recognition, and becomes aware of that Star which encloses his planetary star, just as that star has earlier been seen as enclosing his own tiny "Spark." He thus makes his conscious contact with the solar Logos, and realises within himself the Oneness of all life and manifestation.

This recognition is extended at the seventh initiation, so that two aspects of the One life become realities to the emancipated Buddha.

Thus by a graded series of steps is the initiate brought face to face with Truth and Existence. It will be apparent to thoughtful students why this revealing of the Presence has to precede all other revelations. It produces within the mind of the initiate the following basic realisations:—

His faith for ages is justified, and hope and belief merge themselves in self-ascertained fact. Faith is lost in sight, and things unseen are seen and known. No more can he doubt, but he has become instead, through his own effort, a *knower*.

His oneness with his brothers is proven, and he realises the indissoluble link which binds him to his fellow-men everywhere. Brotherhood is no longer a theory but a proven scientific fact, no more to be disputed than the separateness of men on the physical plane is to be disputed.

The immortality of the soul and the reality of the unseen worlds is for him proven and ascertained. Whereas, before initiation, this belief was based on brief and fleeting vision and strong inner convictions (the result of logical reasoning and of a gradually developing intuition) now it is based on sight and on a recognition past all disproving, of his own immortal nature.

He realises the meaning and source of energy, and can begin to wield power with scientific accuracy and direction. He knows now whence he draws it, and has had a glimpse of the resources of energy which are available. Before, he knew that that energy existed, and used it blindly and sometimes unwisely; now he sees it under the direction of the "open mind," and can co-operate intelligently with the forces of nature.

Thus, in many ways, does the revelation of the Presence produce definite results in the initiate, and thus it is judged by the Hierarchy to be the necessary preamble to all later revelations.

The Revelation of the Vision.

Having brought the initiate face to face with the One with whom for countless ages he has had to do, and having awakened in him an unshakable realisation of the oneness of the fundamental life as it manifests through all lesser lives, the next momentous revelation is that of the Vision. The first revelation has concerned that which is undefinable, illimitable, and (to the finite mind), infinite in its abstractness and absoluteness. The second revelation concerns time and space, and involves the recognition by the initiate—through the newly aroused sense of occult sight—of the part he has played and has to play in the plan, and later of the plan itself in so far as it concerns:—

      a. His Ego.
      b. His egoic group.
      c. His ray group.
      d. His Planetary Logos.

In this fourfold apprehension you have portrayed the gradual realisation that is his during the process of the four initiations preceding final liberation.

At the first initiation he becomes aware definitely of the part, relatively inconspicuous, that he has to play in his personal life during the period ensuing between the moment of revelation and the taking of the second initiation. This may involve one more life or several. He knows the trend they should take, he realises somewhat his share in the service of the race; he sees the plan as a whole where he himself is concerned, a tiny mosaic within the general pattern; he becomes conscious of how he—with his particular type of mind, aggregate of gifts, mental and otherwise, and his varying capacities—can serve, and what must be accomplished by him before he can again stand in the Presence, and receive an extended revelation.

At the second initiation the part his egoic group plays in the general scheme is shown to him. He becomes more aware of the different group units with whom he is intrinsically associated; he realises who they are in their personalities, if in incarnation, and he sees somewhat what are the karmic relations between groups, units and himself; he is given an insight into the specific group purpose, and its relation to other groups. He can now work with added assurance, and his intercourse with people on the physical plane becomes more certain; he can both aid them and himself in the adjusting of karma, and therefore bring about a more rapid approach to the final liberation. Group relations are consolidated, and the plans and purposes can be furthered more intelligently. As this consolidation of group relations proceeds, it produces on the physical plane that concerted action and that wise unity in purpose which results in the materialisation of the higher ideals, and the adaptation of force in the wise furthering of the ends of evolution. When this has reached a certain stage, the units forming the groups have learned to work together, and have thus stimulated each other; they can now proceed to a further expansion of knowledge, resulting in a further capacity to help.

At the third initiation there is revealed to the initiate the purpose of the subray of the ray to which he belongs, that upon which his Ego finds itself. All egoic units are upon some subray of the monadic ray. This knowledge is conferred upon the initiate so as to enable him eventually to find for himself (along the line of least resistance) the ray of his Monad. This subray bears upon its stream of energy many groups of Egos, and the initiate is therefore made aware not only of his egoic group and its intelligent purpose, but of many other groups, similarly composed. Their united energy is working towards a clearly defined goal.

Having learned somewhat group relations, and having developed the ability to work with units in group formation, the initiate now learns the secret of group subordination to the good of the aggregate of groups. This will demonstrate on the physical plane as an ability to work wisely, intelligently and harmoniously with many diverse types, and to co-operate in large plans and wield wide influence.

A part of the plans of the Planetary Logos becomes revealed to him, and the vision includes the revelation of the plan and purpose as it concerns the planet, though as yet the vision is obscured in connection with those plans in their planetary relationship. This brings the initiate through a series of graded realisations to the portals of the fourth initiation. Through the entire loosing of the initiate from all trammels in the three worlds and the breaking of all bonds of limiting karma, the vision this time is greatly extended, and it might be said that for the first time he becomes aware of the extent of planetary purpose and karma within the scheme. His own personal unimportant karma being now adjusted, he can give his attention to the working off of planetary karma, and the far reaching plans of that great Life Who includes all the lesser lives. He not only is brought to a full recognition of the purposes and plans for all the evolutions upon his own planetary scheme, the earth, but also there swings into the radius of his apprehension that planetary scheme which is our earth's complement or polar opposite. He realises the inter-relation existing between the two schemes and the vast dual purpose is revealed to him. It is shown to him how this dual purpose must become one united plan, and henceforth he bends all his energies towards planetary co-operation as it is furthered by work with and through the two great evolutions, human and deva, upon our planet. This concerns the making of adjustments, and the gradual application of energy in stimulation of the various kingdoms in nature, so that through the blending of all of nature's forces the interplay of energy between the two schemes may be quickened. In this way the plans of the solar Logos, as they are being worked out through two Planetary Logoi, may be consummated. The handling, therefore, of solar energy on a tiny scale, is now his privilege, and he is admitted not only into the council chambers of his own Hierarchy, but is permitted entrance also when agents from other planetary schemes are in conference with the Lord of the World and the two great departmental heads.

At the fifth Initiation the vision brings to him a still more extended outlook and a third planetary scheme is seen, forming with the other two schemes one of those triangles of force which are necessitated in the working out of solar evolution. Just as all manifestation proceeds through duality and triplicity back to eventual synthesis so these schemes, which are but centres of force in the body of a solar Logos, work first as separated units living their own integral life, then as dualities, through the interplay of force through any two schemes, thus aiding, stimulating and complementing each other, and finally as a solar triangle, circulating force from point to point and centre to centre until the energy is merged and synthesised and the three work together in unity.

When the adept of the fifth initiation can work in line with the plans of the three Logoi involved, co-operating with Them with ever greater ability, as time elapses, he becomes ready for the sixth Initiation, which admits him to still higher conclaves. He becomes a participant in solar and not merely planetary purposes.

At this sixth Initiation the most marvelous vision of the entire series is his. He sees the solar system as a unit, and gets a brief revealing which opens to his amazed understanding the fundamental purpose of the solar Logos; for the first time he sees the plans as a whole in all their ramifications.

At the seventh Initiation his vision penetrates beyond the solar ring-pass-not, and he sees that which he has long realised as a basic theoretical fact, that our solar Logos is involved in the plans and purposes of a still greater Existence, and that the solar system is but one of many centres of force through which a cosmic Entity vastly greater than our own solar Logos is expressing Himself. In these visions one great purpose underlies them all,—the revelation of essential unity and the unveiling of those inner relationships, which, when known, will tend ever more fully to swing the initiate into the line of self-abnegating service, and which will make of him one who works towards synthesis, towards harmony, and towards a basic unity.

During the Initiation ceremony, the opening of the eyes of the Initiate to see and realise, divides itself into three parts, which are nevertheless parts of one process:—

1. *The past* sweeps before him, and he sees himself playing many parts, all of which are realised to be but the gradual bringing of his forces and capacities to the point where he can be of service to and with his group. He sees and identifies himself—according to the particular initiation—with

    a. Himself in many earlier lives.
    b. His group in earlier groups of lives.
    c. His egoic ray as it pours down through many cycles of time.
    d. His Planetary Logos as He functions in the past through many evolutions and kingdoms in the entire scheme,

and so on until he has identified himself with the past of the one life flowing through all planetary schemes and evolutions in the solar system. This produces in him the resolve to work off karma, and the knowledge (from the seeing of past causes) of how it must be accomplished.

2. *The present.* It is revealed to him what is the specific work to be done during the lesser cycle in which he is immediately involved. This means that he sees not only that which concerns him in any one life, but he knows what is to

be the immediate bit of the plan—involving maybe several of his tiny cycles called lives—which the Planetary Logos seeks to see consummated. He then may be said to know his work past all gainsaying, and can apply himself to his task with a clear knowledge as to the why, the how, and the when.

3. *The future.* Then, for his encouragement, there is granted to him a picture of a final consummation of a glory past all description, with a few outstanding points indicative of the major steps thereto. He sees for one brief second the glory as it shall be, and that path of radiant beauty which shineth ever more and more unto the perfect day. In the earlier stages he sees the glory of his perfected egoic group; later the radiance which pours forth from the ray which carries on its bosom the perfected sons of men of one particular colour and type; later again he gets a glimpse of the perfection of that great Being who is his own Planetary Logos, until finally the perfection of all beauty and the radiance which includes all other rays of light is revealed,—the sun shining in his strength, the solar Logos at the moment of consummated purpose.

CHAPTER XIII

THE RODS OF INITIATION

The Rods of Initiation are of four kinds:—

1. *Cosmic,* used by a cosmic Logos in the initiations of a solar Logos and of the three major Planetary Logoi.

2. *Systemic,* used by a solar Logos in the initiations of a Planetary Logos. With cosmic initiation we have naught to do; it concerns expansions of realisation beyond even the ken of the highest initiate in our solar system. With systemic initiations we are concerned only in trifling measure, for they are on so vast a scale that the average human mind cannot as yet envisage them. Man appreciates these initiations only in so far as they produce effects in the planetary scheme with which he may be concerned. Particularly is this so should the scheme in which he plays his microscopic part be the centre in the Logoic body receiving stimulation. When that is the case, the initiation of his own Planetary Logos takes place, and consequently he (as a cellular body) receives an added stimulation along with the other sons of men.

3. *Planetary,* used by a Planetary Logos for initiatory purposes, and for the third, fourth, and fifth major initiations, with the two higher. At the planetary initiation the Rod of Power, wielded by the solar Logos, is charged with pure electrical force from Sirius, and was received by our Logos during the secondary period of creation, from the hands of that great Entity Who is the presiding Lord of the Lords of Karma. He is the repository of the law during manifestation, and He it is Who is the representative in

the solar system of that greater Brotherhood on Sirius Whose Lodges are found functioning as the occult Hierarchies in the different planets. Again, He it is Who, with the solar Logos to assist Him, invests the various Initiators with power, gives to Them that word in secret which enables Them to draw down the pure electric force with which Their rods of office must be charged, and commits to Their keeping the peculiar secret of Their particular planetary scheme.

4. *Hierarchical*, used by an occult Hierarchy for minor initiations, and for the first two initiations of manas by the Bodhisattva.

When man individualised in Lemurian days, it was through the application of the Rod of Initiation to the Logos of our earth chain, which touched into activity certain centres in His body, with their corresponding groups. This application produced literally the awakening of the life to intelligent work on the mental plane. Animal man was conscious on the physical and on the astral planes. By the stimulation effected by the electric rod this animal man awoke to consciousness on the mental. Thus the three bodies were co-ordinated, and the Thinker enabled to function in them.

All Rods of Initiation cause certain effects:—

a. Stimulation of the latent fires till they blaze.
b. Synthesis of the fires through an occult activity that brings them within the radius of each other.
c. Increase of the vibratory activity of some centre, whether in man, a Heavenly Man, or a solar Logos.
d. Expansion of all the bodies, but primarily of the causal body.
e. The arousing of the kundalinic fire (or the fire at the base of the spine), and the direction of its upward progression. This fire and the fire of manas, are di-

rected along certain routes—or triangles—by the following of the Rod as it moves in a specified manner. There is a definite occult reason, under the laws of electricity, behind the known fact that every initiate presented to the Initiator is accompanied by two of the Masters, Who stand one on either side of the initiate. The three of Them together form a triangle which makes the work possible.

The force of the Rod is twofold, and its power terrific. Apart and alone the initiate could not receive the voltage from the Rod without serious hurt, but in triangular transmission comes safety. We need to remember here that two Masters sponsor all applicants for initiation, and represent two polarities of the electric All. Part of Their function is to stand with applicants for initiation when they come before the Great Lord.

When the rods are held in the hands of the Initiator in His position of power, and at the stated seasons, they act as transmitters of electric force from very high levels, so high indeed that the "Flaming Diamond," at certain of the final initiations, the sixth and seventh, transmits force via the Logos from outside the system altogether. This major Rod is the one used on this planet, but within the system there are several such Rods of Power, and they are to be found in three grades—if it may be so expressed.

One Rod of Initiation is used for the first two initiations, and is wielded by the Great Lord. It is magnetised by the application of the "Flaming Diamond," the magnetisation being repeated for each new World Teacher. There is a wonderful ceremony performed at the time that a new World Teacher takes office, in which He receives His Rod of Power—the same Rod as used since the foundation of our Planetary Hierarchy—and holds it forth to the Lord of the

World, Who touches it with His own mighty Rod, causing a fresh recharging of its electric capacity. This ceremony takes place at Shamballa.

The Rod of Initiation known as the "Flaming Diamond," is used by Sanat Kumara, the One Initiator. This Rod lies hidden "in the East," and holds the fire hidden that irradiates the Wisdom Religion. This Rod was brought by the Lord of the World from Venus, and once in every world period it is subjected to a similar process to that of the lesser Rod, only this time it is recharged by the direct action of the Logos Himself, the Logos of the solar system. The exact location of this Rod is known only to the Lord of the World and to the Chohans of the rays, and being the talisman of this evolution the Chohan of the second ray is—under the Lord of the World—its prime guardian, aided by the deva Lord of the second plane. The Buddhas of Activity are responsible for its custody, and under Them the Chohan of the ray. It is produced only at stated times, when specific work has to be done. It is used not only at the initiating of men, but at certain planetary functions of which nothing is at present known. It has its place and function in certain ceremonies connected with the inner round, and the triangle formed by the Earth, Mars, and Mercury.

The Purpose of the Rods of Power.

In the sceptre of a ruling monarch at this day is hidden the symbolism of these various Rods. They are duly recognised as symbols of office and of power, but it is not generally appreciated that they are of electrical origin, and that their true significance is concerned with the dynamic stimulation of all the subordinates in office who come under their touch, thus inspiring them to increased activity and service for the race.

The great Rod of Power of the Logos Himself is hidden in the sun.

To recapitulate, the esoteric location of the various rods is as follows:—

1. The Rod of the Bodhisattva lies hidden in the "heart of the wisdom," that is, at Shamballa.
2. The Rod of the One Initiator is hidden in "the East," a definite planetary location.
3. The Rod of the solar Logos is hidden in "the heart of the sun," that mysterious subjective sphere which lies back of our physical sun, and of which our physical sun is but the environing shield and envelope.
4. The Rod of the cosmic Logos associated with our solar Logos is secreted in that central spot in the heavens around which our solar system revolves, and which is termed "the central spiritual sun."

One Rod is charged anew at Shamballa for each new World Teacher; the Rod of Sanat Kumara is charged afresh at each recurring world period, and therefore seven times in the history of a planetary scheme. The Logoic Rod of Power is electrified at the recurrence of each new period of creation, or for each solar system through which the Logos manifests, as a man manifests through his physical body life. The first two ceremonies take place at Shamballa, the sacred point of planetary manifestation, that central location in our physical planet which corresponds to the heart of a human being. Many of the places on the earth's surface, for instance, which are famed for their healing properties, are thus noted because they are magnetised spots, and their magnetic properties demonstrate as healing influences. The recognition of these properties by man is but the preamble of a later and more definite recognition, which will eventuate when his etheric sight is normally developed.

These magnetic spots are magnetised in three ways:—

1. By Sanat Kumara working through the Manu. This occurs when it is desirable to form a central magnetic point which, by its attractive power, will draw into a coherent whole some race, nation, or large organisation. Every nation has its "magnetic point," formed in etheric matter by the application of the "Flaming Diamond" to the ethers; it is the national heart and the basis of the national character. Usually the chief city of a nation is built up around it, but this is not invariably so.

2. By Sanat Kumara working through the Bodhisattva. In this case, the electric force in the Rod is wielded in order to draw closer together those influences which demonstrate in the great religions of the world. The lesser Rod of Power is used here in conjunction with the greater. By their means the attractive quality or keynote of any religion is struck, and of any organisation with a religious basis.

3. By Sanat Kumara working through the Mahachohan. By the wielding of the Rod of Power the magnetic focal points of those great organisations which affect the civilisation and the culture of a people are brought into coherent activity.

All physical plane organisation—governmental, religious, or cultural—is the working out of inner forces and causes, and, before they definitely appear in physical manifestation, a focalisation—if it might be so expressed—of these influences and energies, takes place on etheric levels. The organisation of the Freemasons is a case in point. It has two magnetic centres, one of which is in Central Europe. In all the cases cited, the Lord of the World was the officiating agent, as is ever the case in the founding of great and impor-

tant movements. In all lesser movements for the helping of
the race, initiated by the Masters working through Their
disciples, the aid of the Bodhisattva is invoked, and the lesser
Rod of Power employed.

When disciples initiate a movement on a relatively tiny
scale, the Master with Whom they work can similarly assist
them, and though He wields no Rod of Power, He has
methods whereby He can stimulate and cause to cohere the
little endeavour of the faithful followers. Thus in all
departments of human life the Rods of Initiation and the
Words of Power are used. The entire world government
functions under law and order, and the whole scheme is
interdependent.

To return to the subject of human initiation, and these
Rods of Power. At the time of the Initiation ceremony,
after the two great revelations there comes a moment of
utter silence, and in the interim the initiate realises within
himself the meaning of *"Peace."* He stands, as it were, in
a void, or in a vacuum, wherein naught seemingly can reach
him; he stands betwixt earth and heaven for a brief second, conscious of naught but the meaning of things as
they are, realising his own essential divinity, and the part
which he must play when he again returns to earth service from the Council Chamber of Heaven. He is conscious
of no anxiety, fear, or doubt. He has contacted the divine
"Presence," and has seen the vision. He knows what he has
to do and how he must do it, and peace and joy unutterable
fill his heart. This is an interlude of stillness before a
period of renewed activity, which begins at the moment that
the Rod is applied. Whilst he has been thus withdrawn
within himself, with all his forces centred in his heart, the
attendant Lodge of Masters have been performing certain
ceremonies and chanting certain words, preparatory to the
appearance of the Initiator upon the throne, and the wielding

of the Rod. The Hierophant has hitherto been present, but the work has been handled by the Lodge and the Sponsors. He now ascends to the place of power, and the Rod is brought to Him by its legitimate custodians.

It is not possible here to publish the details of the next stage, beyond using the description as embodied in the words "fire descends from heaven." Through the utterance of certain words and phrases, which are one of the secrets of initiation, and which vary with each initiation, the electrical force to be employed descends upon the Rod, passing through the heart and the hand of the Initiator to the *Three* Who stand in triangular relation to the throne of office. They receive it in turn, and circulate it by act of will through Their hearts, thus passing it to the Sponsors. They again, by an act of will, prepare to transmit it to that centre in the body of the Initiate which is (according to the initiation) to receive stimulation. Then succeeds an interesting interlude, wherein the united wills of the Hierarchy are blended in order to transmit that force which the Rod has put into circulation. The Hierophant utters the word, and the force is literally thrown into the initiate's bodies and centres, passing down through the centres on the mental plane, via the astral centres, to the centres on etheric levels, which finally absorb it. This is the stupendous moment for the initiate, and brings to him a realisation of the literal absolute truth of the phrase that "God is a consuming fire." He knows past all gainsaying that fiery energy and electric force constitute the sumtotal of all that is. He is literally bathed in the fires of purification; he sees fire on all sides, pouring out through the Rod, circulating around the Triangle, and passing through the bodies of the two sponsoring adepts. For a brief second, the entire Lodge of Masters and initiates, standing in Their ceremonial places without the Triangle, are hidden from view by a wall of pure fire. The initiate sees no one, save the Hierophant, and is aware of nothing but a fiery blaze of pure, blue-white flame, which burns, but destroys not, which intensifies the activity of every atom in his body without disintegrating, and which purifies his entire nature. The fire tries his work, of what sort it is, and he passes through the Flame.

The Effect of the Application of the Rod.

A. *Upon the Initiate's bodies:* The effect is four-fold and lasting, but varies according to the initiation taken. The action of the Rod is most carefully and scientifically regulated, and at each succeeding initiation the voltage is increased, and the activity of the resulting fire and its heat intensified. By the application of the Rod the initiate finds:—

1. That the activity of each individual atom in the various bodies is increased, resulting in a greater degree of nervous energy and an elasticity and resistance which will serve him in good stead in the strenuous life of service ahead.

2. That matter of an undesirable type in his bodies is shaken loose, and the atomic wall somewhat destroyed, making the atoms radioactive—if it might be so expressed—and therefore more easily eliminated.

3. The fires of the body are stimulated, and the total energy of the threefold lower man is co-ordinated, so that there is less waste of energy and a greater coherence and uniformity in action.

4. The aligning of the various bodies in connection with the causal, or egoic body is aided, and thus continuity of consciousness, and receptivity to the behests of the Ego, become possible.

The initiate will find, when he returns from the ceremony, and takes up his work in the world, that the stimulation received will bring about in his bodies a period of
great activity, and also of strife. This strife, persisted in to
the point of victory, will result in his taking out of his body
undesirable matter, and building in new and better material;
he will find that his powers for service are enormously increased, and his nervous energy intensified, so that he can
draw upon reserves of force in service hitherto unsuspected.
He will find, also, that the response of the physical brain
to the voice of the higher Self, and its receptivity to the
higher and subtler impressions, is greatly furthered. Eventually, through the work accomplished, he will succeed in
eliminating all matter of a subatomic character, and will
then build bodies of substance of the highest subplane on
each plane; he will become aware that all his energies can
be consciously and constructively controlled, that he knows
the real meaning of continuity of consciousness, and can
function simultaneously on the three planes with full inner
realisation.

B. *Upon the causal or egoic body*.

It is only possible to touch very briefly upon the effect
of the application of the Rod to the causal body of the
initiate. The subject is immense, and will be more fully
dealt with in *A Treatise on Cosmic Fire*. There are just two
ways in which some idea of the fundamental truth will be
conveyed to the mind of the student, which we might now
consider.

First, the student should bear in mind the interesting
significance of the fact that he, on the physical plane, is a
functioning personality, with known and realised characteristics, and yet withal, that he is a subjective Life, who

uses that personality as a medium of expression, and who—through the agency of the physical, emotional, and mental bodies which comprise the threefold lower man—makes his contacts with the physical plane and thus develops. The same general idea of development must be now extended to the higher Self, the Ego on its own plane. This Ego is a great solar angel, who is the medium of expression for the Monad or pure spirit, just as is the personality for the Ego on the lower level. From the point of view of man in the three worlds, this Ego, or Solar Lord, is eternal; he persists throughout the entire cycle of incarnations, just as the personality persists during the tiny physical life cycle. Nevertheless, this period of existence is only relatively permanent, and the day dawns when the life which expresses itself through the medium of the Ego, the Thinker, the Solar Lord or Manasadeva, seeks to loose itself from even this limitation, and to return to the source from which it originally emanated.

The life then, which manifested as a solar angel, and which, through inherent energy, held together through long ages the form egoic, withdraws itself gradually, and the form slowly dissipates; the lesser lives of which it has been constituted, return to the general fount of deva substance, plus the increased consciousness and activity which is theirs through the experience of being built into a form, and utilised by a still higher aspect of existence. Similarly, in the case of the personality, when the life egoic withdraws, the threefold lower self dissipates; the little lives which form the body of what has been called the lunar self (in contradistinction to the solar self, being but its reflection) are absorbed into the general reservoir of deva substance of a lower vibration to that which composed the body egoic. Similarly, also, their evolution has been furthered through having been built into a form for the use of the higher Self.

Through the application of the Rod of Initiation, the work of separating the spiritual self from the higher self is furthered, and the imprisoned life gradually escapes, whilst the causal body is slowly absorbed or dissipated.

This has led to the expression, sometimes used in occult books, of "the cracking of the causal body" at each initiation, and to the idea of the inner central fire gradually breaking through and destroying the confining walls, and also of the destruction of the Temple of Solomon through the withdrawal of the Shekinah. All these phrases are symbolic wordings, and are attempts to convey to the mind of man fundamental truth from different angles.

By the time the fourth initiation has been reached, the work of destruction is accomplished, the solar angel returns to his own place, having performed his function, and the solar lives seek their point of emanation. The life within the form mounts up then in triumph to the bosom of its "Father in Heaven," just as the life within the physical body at the moment of death seeks its source, the Ego, and this likewise in four stages:—

1. By the withdrawal from the dense physical body.
2. By the withdrawal from the etheric body.
3. By a later vacating of the astral body.
4. A final leaving of the mental body.

Another way of emphasising the same truth is to regard the egoic body as a centre of force, a wheel of energy, or a lotus, and to picture it as a lotus with nine petals, hiding within these petals a central unit of three petals; these in their turn secrete the central life, or the "jewel in the lotus." As evolution proceeds, these three circles of three petals gradually unfold, having a simultaneous effect on one or other of the central three. These three circles are called respectively the petals of Sacrifice, Love, and Knowledge. At initiation the Rod is applied to the petals in a scientific manner, and regulated according to ray and tendency. This brings about the opening of the central bud, the revelation of the jewel, the withdrawal of that jewel from the casket which has so long shielded it, and its transference to "the crown," as it is occultly called, meaning its return to the Monad whence it came.

We must clearly recognise that all the above is but an attempt, through the limiting agency of words, to describe the method and the rites whereby spiritual liberation is finally achieved in this cycle; first, through the method of evolutionary unfoldment, or gradual development, and then in the final stages through the Rod of Initiation.

C. *Upon the centres.*

At the time that initiation is taken, the centres are all active, and the lower four (which correspond to the Personality) are beginning the process of translating the fire into the three higher. The dual revolution in the lower centres is clearly to be seen, and the three higher are commencing to be similarly active. By the application of the Rod of Initiation at the time of the initiation ceremony, definite results are achieved in connection with the centres, which might be enumerated as follows:—

The fire at the base of the spine is definitely directed to whichever centre is the object of special attention. This varies according to ray, or the specialised work of the initiate.

The centre has its activity intensified, its rate of revolution increased, and certain of the central spokes of the wheel brought into more active radiance. These spokes of the wheel, or these petals of the lotus, have a close connection with the different spirillae in the permanent atoms, for instance, and in their stimulation comes into play one or more of the corresponding spirillae in the permanent atoms on the three lower planes. After the third initiation a corresponding stimulation takes place in the permanent atoms of the Triad, leading to a co-ordination of the buddhic vehicle, and the transference of the lower polarisation into the higher.

By the application of the Rod of Initiation, the downflow of force from the Ego to the personality is tripled, the direction of that force being dependent upon whether the centres receiving attention are the etheric or the astral at the first and second initiations, or whether the initiate is standing before the Lord of the World. In the latter case, his mental centres, or their corresponding force vortices on higher levels, will receive stimulation. When the World Teacher initiates at the first and second initiations, the direction of the triadal force is turned to the vivification of the heart and throat centres in their position of synthesising the lower. When the One Initiator applies the Rod of His power, the downflow is from the Monad, and though the throat and heart intensify vibration as a response, the main direction of the force is to the seven head centres, and finally (at liberation) to the radiant head centre above, synthesising the lesser seven head centres.

The centres, at initiation, receive a fresh access of vibratory capacity and of power, and this results in the exoteric life as:—

1. A sensitiveness and refinement of the vehicles which may result at first in much suffering to the initiate, but which produce a capacity to respond, that far outweighs the incidental pain.

2. A development of psychic faculty that again may lead to temporary distress, but which eventually causes a recog nition of the one self in all selves, which is the goal of endeavour.

3. A burning away of the etheric web, through the grad ual arousing of kundalini and its correct geometrical progression, and a resultant continuity of consciousness that enables the initiate consciously to utilise *time* as a factor on the planes of evolution.

4. A gradual grasp of the law of vibration as an aspect of the basic law of building, the law of attraction, is brought about, and the initiate learns consciously to build, to manipulate thought matter for the perfecting of the plans of the Logos, to work in mental essence, and to apply the law on mental levels, and thereby affect the physical plane. Motion originates cosmically on cosmic levels, and in the microcosm the same will be seen. There is an occult hint here that, pondered on, will reveal much. At initiation, at the moment of the application of the Rod, the initiate *consciously* realises the meaning of the Law of Attraction in form building, and in the synthesis of the three fires. Upon his ability to retain that realisation, and himself to apply the law, will depend his power to progress.

5. The Hierophant transmits higher manasic energy to the initiate, so that he is enabled consciously to know and recognise the plan for his group centre, through the immensely increased stimulation. This force descends from the manasic permanent atom via the antahkarana, and is directed to whichever centre the Hierophant—under the law—sees should be stimulated.

6. The Initiator stabilises the force and regulates its flow, as it circulates through the egoic body, so that when the work of unfoldment is accomplished, the seventh prin-

ciple at the Heart of the Lotus can stand revealed. After each initiation the lotus is more unfolded, and light from the centre begins to blaze forth—a light or fire which ultimately burns through the three enshrining petals, and permits the full inner glory to be seen, and the electric fire of spirit to be manifested. As this is brought about on the second subplane of the mental plane (whereon the egoic lotus is now situated) a corresponding stimulation takes place in the dense substance which forms the petals or wheels of the centres on the astral and etheric levels.

CHAPTER XIV

THE ADMINISTRATION OF THE OATH

The Work of the Lodge during Initiation.

We now come to the most solemn part of the initiation ceremony. This ceremony, from one point of view, divides itself into three parts:—

First. That in which the initiate is concerned and in which he realises his own august Self, the Presence, and sees the vision and the plan.

Second. That in which the Initiator is concerned, in which He wields the Rod of Fire, and effects certain specific results in the body of the applicant.

Third. That in which certain words and formulas are committed to the initiate by the Hierophant, and which he carries away within his consciousness in order the better to carry out that portion of the plan which concerns himself.

During the whole procedure the Lodge of Masters, congregated without the Triangle of force, has been occupied with a three-fold work, Their aim being to produce certain results in the consciousness of the initiate and thus to aid the Hierophant in His strenuous endeavour. It must be remembered that under the law of economy wherever there is an application or a transmission of force from one force centre to another there is a consequent diminution in the centre of withdrawal. This is the basis of the set times and seasons in connection with the initiation ceremony. The sun is the source of all energy and power, and the work of the Initiator is facilitated when advantage is taken of favourable solar conditions. The times and seasons are ascertained through esoteric solar and cosmic astrology; this being based, of course, on the correct figures, the true mathematical conception, and a real knowledge of the basic facts concerning the planets and the solar system. The horoscope of the initiate is also invariably cast so as to check the time for an individual initiation, and only when the individual signs blend and coincide with the ceremonial chart by which the Initiator is guided, is it possible to perform the ceremony. This is the reason why sometimes initiation has to be postponed to a later life, even when the initiate has done the necessary work.

The threefold work of the Lodge during the ceremony may be described as follows:—

First: The chanting of certain mantrams sets loose energy from a particular planetary centre. It must be remembered here that every planetary scheme is a centre in the body of a Solar Logos, and embodies a peculiar type of energy or force. According to the energy desired at a particular initiation, so it is transferred, via the sun, from that planetary centre to the initiate. The procedure is as follows:—

a. The energy is set in motion from the planetary centre through the power of the Planetary Logos, aided by the scientific knowledge of the Lodge, and the utilisation of certain words of power.

b. It passes thence to the sun where it mingles with pure solar energy.

c. It is transmitted from the sun to that particular chain in our Earth scheme which corresponds numerically to the particular originating planetary scheme.

d. From there it is transferred to the corresponding globe, and thence to the dense physical planet. By the use of a particular mantram the Initiator then focuses the energy in His own body, using it both as a receiving and a transmitting station. Eventually it reaches the initiate, via the Triangle and the Sponsors. It will be apparent, therefore, to the student that when the Initiator is the Lord of the World, or the physical reflection of the Planetary Logos of our scheme, the force comes more directly to the initiate than at the first two initiations, wherein the Bodhisattva is the Hierophant. Only at the third initiation will the initiate be in a condition to receive *direct* planetary force.

Second: The concentration undertaken by the Lodge assists the initiate to realise within himself the various processes undergone. This is accomplished by working definitely on his mental body, and thus stimulating all the atoms, through the united thought power of the Masters. The work of apprehension is thus directly aided. This concentration in no way resembles hypnotic suggestion, or the powerful impress of stronger minds upon the weaker. It takes the form of a strenuous meditation by the assembled Masters and initiates upon the realities concerned and upon the Self; through the force thus liberated the initiate is enabled to transfer his consciousness more easily away from the not-self to the divine essentials wherewith he is immediately concerned. The thought power of the Masters succeeds in shutting out the vibration of the three worlds and enables the applicant literally to "leave behind him" all the past and to have that far-seeing vision which sees the end from the beginning and the things of time as though they were not.

Third: Through certain ceremonial rhythmic action the

Lodge greatly assists in the work of initiation. Just as in the Wesak Festival, results in force demonstration are brought about by the use of chanted mantrams and the sacred ceremonial pacing and interweaving of the assembled crowd in the formation of geometrical figures, so in the initiation ceremony a similar procedure is followed. The geometrical figures appropriate for the various initiations differ, and herein lies one of the safeguards of the ceremony. The initiate knows the set figure for his own initiation, but no more.

All these three aspects of the work of the Masters and initiates in Lodge assembled, occupy them until the moment when the Rod has been applied. Through its application the initiate has become a member of the Lodge, and the entire ceremonial then changes, prior to the taking of the oath and the revelation of the Word and Secret.

The Sponsors drop back from either side of the initiate and take Their places in the ranks, whilst the three Buddhas of Activity (or Their representatives at the first two initiations) take Their stand behind the seat of office of the Hierophant. The Lodge members are grouped differently, and initiates of the same degree as the newly admitted applicant place themselves around him, and assist in the final part of the ceremony; the remainder of the initiates and adepts stand in their various grades.

The earlier three stages of the initiation ceremony are the same for all initiations. In the final two stages those who are not of equal rank with the newly made initiate (such as first degree initiates at the initiation of a third degree member) drop back to the rear of the Hall of Initiation at Shamballa, and a "wall of silence" is built up through mantric energy between the two groups; a vacuum, so to speak, is formed, and nothing can then be transmitted from the inner group to the outer. The latter confine themselves to deep meditation and the chanting of certain formulas, and in the inner group around the Hierophant a dual performance is taking place:—

a. The newly made initiate is taking the oath.
b. Certain Words and Secrets are being handed over to him.

Two Types of Oaths.

All oaths connected with the occult Hierarchy may be divided into two groups:—

1. *The Oath of Initiation,* in which the initiate binds himself by the most solemn pledges never to reveal, on pain of summary punishment, any occult secret, or to express in words outside the Initiation Hall that which has been committed to his keeping.
2. *The Oath of Office,* administered when any member of the Lodge takes a specific post in Hierarchical work. This oath deals with his functions and with his relations to

    a. The Lord of the World,
    b. His immediate superior,
    c. His fellow workers in the Lodge,
    d. The world of men whom he is to serve.

It is needless to say more here regarding this latter type of oath, as it concerns only officials of the Hierarchy.

The Oath of Initiation.

The Oath of Initiation, with which we are dealing now, is divided into three sections, and is administered by the Hierophant to the initiate, being repeated after the Initiator phrase by phrase; it is punctuated at various points by the chanting, by initiates of the same degree, of words in Sensa equivalent to "So let it be."

The three divisions of the oath may be roughly described as:—

1. A solemn phrase embodying the purpose actuating the initiate, a protestation as to his unchangeable will-attitude, and a solemn declaration as to his realisation, coupled with a promise to reveal no part of the realised purpose except in so far as his daily life in the world of men and his service for the race will proclaim it. This involves an oath as to secrecy concerning the revealed part of the Logoic plan seen in the "revelation of the vision."

2. An undertaking of a profoundly solemn nature concerning his relation to his other selves, the Lodge of which he is a member, and the selves of men everywhere. This involves his attitude to his brothers of all degrees, and includes also a serious undertaking never to reveal the true nature of the Self aspect as it has been shown to him in initiation. This includes an oath of secrecy as to the realised relationship of the Solar Logos to the Planetary Logos, and of the Planetary Logos of our scheme to the scheme itself.

3. The enunciation of a solemn undertaking never to reveal to anyone the knowledge that has come to him as to the sources of energy and of force with which he has been brought into contact. This is a triple oath to retain complete silence as to the true nature of energy, as to its laws of manipulation, and a pledge only to use the force placed at his disposal through initiation for the service of the race and the furthering of the plans of the Planetary Logos.

This great oath is couched in different terms, according to the initiation undergone, and, as earlier said, is taken in three sections with an interlude between each part occupied by certain ceremonial work of the initiated group around the newly admitted brother.

It might here be noted that each section of the oath really concerns one of the three aspects of divine manifestation, and as the initiate takes his pledge, one of the three Heads of Departments collaborates with the Initiator in the work of administration. In this way energy of a triple nature becomes available according to the different sections of the oath taken. This energy flows down from the three major rays, through the Hierophant and the corresponding departmental head at the first two initiations, to the initiate, via the group of initiates of the same degree, so that each initiation is a means of stimulation and expansion to all. At the final five initiations the force flows via the three Buddhas of Activity instead of the departmental heads.

It might be of interest to point out here that during this part of the ceremony the group is bathed in colour, corresponding to the type of energy and its originating planetary scheme, and it is the work of the Initiator to put the initiate in touch with this energy. This pours down upon the group from the moment that segregation has been effected, and is brought about by the Initiator using certain words and elevating His Rod of Power. The three Buddhas of Activity, Who are the great energy centres upon our planet, then touch the tip of the Rod with Their staffs of office, a certain mystic Word is jointly uttered by Them, and the downpour begins, continuing to the end of the ceremony.

The question may be asked whether any initiates break their oath. Very rarely, for we must remember that no initiation is taken until a certain stage has been reached. A few cases have occurred, but as the Lord of the World is cognisant of all that transpires, the future, as well as the present and the past, no opportunity is ever given to an initiate to reveal that which is hidden. Intent may exist, but opportunity will lack. The initiate who thus sins in intention will be struck dumb, and sometimes dead, prior to thus failing.

CHAPTER XV

THE GIVING OF THE WORD

The Solar Words.

The basis of all manifested phenomena is the enunciated sound, or the Word spoken with power, that is, with the full purpose of the will behind it. Herein, as is known, lies the value of meditation, for meditation produces eventually that inner dynamic purpose and recollection, or that internal ideation which must invariably precede the uttering of any creative sound. When it is said that the Logos produced the worlds through meditation it means that within His own centre of consciousness there was a period wherein He brooded over and meditated upon the purposes and plans He had in view; wherein He visualised to Himself the entire world process as a perfected whole, seeing the end from the beginning and being aware of the detail of the consummated sphere. Then, when His meditation was concluded, and the whole completed as a picture before His inner vision, He brought into use a certain Word of Power which had been committed to Him by the *One about Whom naught may be said,* the Logos of the cosmic scheme of which our system is but a part. With cosmic and Logoic initiations we are not concerned, except in so far as the human initiations reflect their stupendous prototypes, but it is of interest to the student to realise that just as at each initiation some Word of Power is committed to the initiate, so similarly to the Logos was committed the great Word of Power which produced our solar system, that Word which is called the

"Sacred Word," or AUM. It must be here remembered that this sound AUM is man's endeavour to reproduce on an infinitesimally small scale the cosmic triple sound whereby creation was made possible. The Words of Power of all degrees have a triple sequence.

First. They are sounded by some fully *selfconscious* entity, and this invariably takes place after a period of deliberation or meditation wherein the purpose in toto is visualised.

Second. They affect the deva kingdom and produce the creation of forms. This effect is dual in character—

a. The devas on the evolutionary path, the great builders of the solar system, and those under them who have passed the human stage respond to the sound of the Word, and with conscious realisation collaborate with the one who has breathed it forth, and thus the work is carried out.

b. The devas on the involutionary arc, the lesser builders, who have not passed through the human stage, also respond to the sound, but unconsciously, or perforce, and through the power of the initiated vibrations build the required forms out of their own substance.

Third. They act as a stabilising factor, and as long as the force of the sound persists, the forms cohere. When the Logos, for instance, finishes the sounding of the sacred AUM, and the vibration ceases, then disintegration of the forms will ensue. So with the Planetary Logos, and thus on down the scale.

The Words of Power, or the permutations of the AUM, exist in every possible tone, sub-tone, and quarter-tone, and upon these shades of sound the work of creation and its sustentation is built up. A multiplicity of sounds exists within each greater sound and affects different groups. It must be remembered also that, generally and broadly speaking, the sounds within the solar system fall into two groups:—

1. *The initiatory sounds,* or those which produce manifestation or phenomena of any kind on all planes.

2. *Eventuating sounds,* or those which are produced from within the forms themselves during the evolutionary process, and which are the aggregate of the tones of every form in any particular kingdom of nature. Every form likewise has a tone which is produced by the minute sounds produced by the atoms composing that form. These sounds grow out of the other group and affect inferior groups or kingdoms, if the word "inferior" may be used in connection with any department of divine manifestation. For instance, the human kingdom (the fourth creative Hierarchy) was produced by a triple AUM sounded in a particular key by the three persons of the Trinity in unison,—God the Father, God the Son, and God the Holy Spirit, or Shiva, Vishnu, and Brahma. This sound is still going forth; the interplay and interblending of the many tiny notes of each human being produces a great united sound which can be heard in the high places and which, in its turn, is having a definite effect upon the animal kingdom. It is one of the factors which produces animal forms, both for human and animal occupation, for it must ever be remembered that man links the animal and the divine.

It is neither possible nor desirable to enumerate the Words of Power, but certain general indications may be given which will help the student to realise somewhat the magnitude of the subject and its intricacy.

1. The Great Word, as sounded by the Logos of the solar system, and communicated to Him by His superior.

2. Three Words committed by the Solar Logos to each of the three Logoi as follows:—

   a. The sacred sound A to Shiva, He Who embodies the spirit or will aspect. It is the Word through which God the Father works.

   b. The sound U to Vishnu, God the Son. He is the form-builder and provides the body which the spirit must occupy, thereby making divine incarnation possible. A is the life sound, U is the form sound.

   c. The sound M to Brahma, Who, in His work of Energy-provider, links in active intelligence, spirit and form, or the self and not-self.

It might here be pointed out that much information anent the three departments of the Hierarchy of our planet will come to the student who wisely ponders these functions.

3. Seven Great Words, again based on the sacred three sounds A U M . These produced creation, or the manifestation of the seven planes of our solar system. They are committed not to human entities, but to the seven great Devas or Raja-Lords who are the ensouling lives of a plane; hence in the various initiations their collaboration is necessary, before these key words can be committed to the initiate.

4. Forty-nine Words related to the forty-nine subplanes or Fires. These again are committed to the forty-nine Builders of the Sacred Fires.

The above two groups of words are in the jurisdiction of the third aspect, and are given out by Brahma.

5. There are again five Great Words with signs which come under the department of Vishnu, or God the Son,

and are breathed out by Him. By their means the five king-doms of nature on the evolutionary arc came into being:—

> a. The mineral kingdom.
> b. The vegetable kingdom.
> c. The animal kingdom.
> d. The human kingdom.
> e. The spiritual kingdom.

These five are permutations of, or are built up upon the sound U, as the ones earlier enumerated are built up upon the sound M.

In connection with the first three kingdoms it may be of interest to note that they are based upon two sounds, the U sounded on the basic key tone of the M. In the fourth kingdom the M tone is dying down and the two notes sounded forth are the U and the A. In the fifth king-dom the M has subsided into a distant undertone, the U is blended with it so as to be indistinguishable, and the A, or Shiva note, is pealing forth in power, and is practically the only note heard. By the sounding of this note,—that of Shiva the Destroyer,—the not-self is negated, and all that is not of spirit passes into dissolution. It is the coming in of the A sound which affects the severance or liberation of the initiate from the three worlds.

6. There are certain Words also committed to each of the Planetary Logoi, and they are the basis of planetary manifestation. As is well known, the sound of the Brahma aspect, or the third aspect of our particular Planetary Logos, is FA, and herein lies much of illumination as to His point in evolution, for it is immediately apparent that the A sound is reaching even the dense physical.

7. Within our own Hierarchy there are numbers of Words built up upon the Great Word of our Planetary Lo-gos, and these are committed to the Departmental Heads,

who in turn pass them on in permutated order to the graded initiates. It will be wise here for the student to differentiate carefully in his mind between *words* and *sounds,* for the word veils the thought or intended idea or purpose, and the sound makes it possible to manifest in matter of some kind, on one or other of the seven planes.

We cannot here trace the expansion of the basic words, from their enunciation by cosmic entities down to the infinitesimal differentiations produced in the speech of man, the vocal expression of the animals, and the song of birds. Each is a manifestation of consciousness in some degree, and each produces an effect. What the initiate is learning to do is to make sounds *consciously,* and thus produce a studied and desired result; to utter words, and be fully aware of the consequence on all planes; and to create forms and direct energy through sacred sounds, and thus further the ends of evolution.

It has been necessary to digress thus before taking up the committal of words to the initiate, in order to emphasise the radical importance of the matter, and thus account for the carefully guarding of this aspect of divine work.

The Use of the Words.

We have already dealt with the significance of the Words of Power in a brief manner. We might now sum up certain of the inferred postulates, and then touch somewhat upon the initiation ceremony, and the Words as committed to the initiate. The postulates here made are nine in number, and if duly pondered upon by the aspirant, will reveal to him much anent the creative process and the power of speech.

1. All the Words of Power are rooted in the Great Word committed to the Solar Logos at the dawn of manifestation.

2. All the Words of Power are permutations or expansions of the three basic sounds, and increase in length as the planes are involved, until the sentences and speech of the finite unit, man, in their myriad differentiations are arrived at.

3. Therefore, on the path of return, speech becomes ever more brief, words are more sparingly used, and the time eventually comes when the adept employs formulas of words only as required to carry out specific purposes along two lines:—

> a. Definite creative processes.
> b. Specific direction of energy.

This, of course, on the planes in the three worlds.

4. The aspirant, therefore, has mainly three things to do when preparing for initiation:—

> a. To control every activity of his threefold lower nature. This involves the application of intelligent energy to every atom of his three sheaths—physical, astral, and mental. It is literally the shining forth of the Brahma, or third aspect, of the inner God.
> b. To control his speech every minute of every day. This is a statement easily made, but most difficult to make practical. He who achieves it is rapidly nearing emancipation. This applies not to the reticence, the moroseness, the silence, and the voicelessness which often distinguishes natures but little evolved, and which are in reality an inarticulate condition. It refers to the controlled use of words to effect certain ends, and the retention of speech energy when not needed,— a very different matter. It involves a realisation of cycles; of times and of seasons; it supposes a knowledge of the power of sound, and of the effects produced

through the spoken word; it involves an apprehension of the building forces of nature and their due manipulation, and is based on an ability to wield mental matter, and to set it in motion, in order to produce results in physical matter, consonant with the clearly defined purpose of the inner God. It is the shining forth of the second aspect of the Self, the Vishnu, or form-building aspect, which is the prime characteristic of the Ego on its own plane. It would be well to ponder on this.

c. To meditate, and thus arrive at the purpose of the Ego. By thus meditating the first aspect comes steadily into greater prominence, and the conscious will of the inner God can make itself felt on the physical plane.

The three activities of the aspirant must parallel each other, and it will be noted that the second is the outcome of the first and will manifest as energy on the physical plane. Only when the aspirant has made real progress in these three lines of endeavour will the first of the Great Words be committed to him.

5. Every Great Word includes within itself its differentiations, its expansions and permutations, and by its utterance the initiate sets in motion the lesser, through the vibration of the greater. Hence the terrific responsibility and the magnitude of the results achieved. Each Word is committed to the initiate orally and visually. It is spoken to him first in the form of seven syllables, each of which he has to memorise as a separate Word. Then he is shown how to blend these seven so as to make a threefold sound and thus produce more united and far reaching results. Finally the three are blended into one Word which is committed to him. The seven words which form the Great Word at any initiation are communicated to the initiate by the initiates of equal rank with his own. This group divides itself into

seven groups, according to subray or ray formation, and each group then chants one word in rapid rotation. Simultaneously, the colours and symbols of the various sounds pass in front of him, so that he hears and sees that which is committed to him. The more advanced group around the throne of office (the three Departmental Heads at the first two initiations, and the Pratyeka Buddhas at the final ones) chant then for him the triple Word which blends the seven, and again he sees it before his inner eye. Finally the Initiator sounds it forth, and the initiate becomes aware within himself, in practical experience, of the one great sound, and knows in one particular centre what its vibration is. As is well known, every centre is connected with some plane, scheme, ray, and other septenary divisions, and thus the significance of its inner reaction will be apparent.

6. The Masters and initiates, in Their work of aiding the evolution of the three worlds, concern Themselves principally with the seven syllables of the Word of Their degree or initiated grade. The three Words which blend the seven are seldom used except under the direct sanction of one of the departmental heads (according to the syllable involved each Word is directly connected with the triple AUM, and therefore with the Brahma, Vishnu, or Siva aspect, of which the three Heads are the planetary representatives).

When any initiate desires to use, for evolutionary purposes, the entire Word as a unit, the sanction of the assembled Lodge has to be gained, for such a Word affects the matter of an entire plane within a planetary scheme, and consequently the matter of those planes which are subsidiary to the one involved. For instance, an initiate of the third degree, in sounding the Word of his degree, affects the matter of the lower mental subplanes, and subsequently the matter of the astral and physical planes. An initiate of the second degree similarly affects the astral plane, and subsequently the physical. Far reaching results are thus achieved, and the work of many is thus affected.

7. Every Word, differentiated or synthesised, affects the deva kingdoms, and hence the form-building aspects of manifestation. No sound is ever made without producing a corresponding response in deva substance, and driving multitudes of tiny lives to take specific forms. These forms persist and carry out their functions just as long as the sound which caused them is prolonged, and the specific will-energy of the one who initiated the sound is directed towards the living form. This is equally true of a Solar Logos enunciating the AUM, and thus producing the solar system; of a Planetary Logos sounding his planetary Word, and producing a planetary scheme; of an adept producing results for the helping of humanity on the physical plane; and of an ordinary human being, who—in much differentiated diversified speech—expresses an inner purpose or state of mind, and thus builds a form or vehicle in deva substance. The majority of human beings as yet build unconsciously, and the form constructed is either of a beneficent or maleficent agency, according to the underlying motive or purpose of the man, and will carry out his will as long as its term of being persists.

8. Every Word sounded is distinguished by:—

    a. A specific colour.

    b. A particular tone.

    c. A special form.

    d. A degree of energy or activity.

    e. The nature of the ensouling life, self-conscious, conscious, or unconscious, God, man, or deva.

The student, again, will find this equally true of a solar system, of a planetary scheme, of a human being, of a thought form ensouled by an elemental life, and of the atom of the physicist or chemist. In the knowledge of these facts, and in their conscious realisation, may be known the true occultist. The Solar Logos sounded forth a Word, the form of our solar system came into being, its color being blue and its note a particular cosmic musical tone. Its degree of activity is of a specific mathematical notation beyond the grasp of the human mind at this stage of development; and the nature of its great ensouling Life, that of the triple Logos, is active, intelligent Love.

9. The Great Word of our solar system keys in, if it might be so expressed, with other Words, and is but one Word of the sevenfold Word, known to that great Existence Who stands in the same relation to the Solar Logos as the latter does to the Planetary Logos. The sacred Words of seven solar systems (of which ours is but one) make up this septenary sound, which vibrates at this time in the cosmic spheres.

In these nine statements are very cursorily summed up the major truths anent the creative processes in the solar system. In them lies hidden the secret of the true magic, and in their comprehension will come to the man who has spiritual intuition, purity of life and motive, altruistic intention, and a stern self-control and courage, the power to further the purposes of the Ego, who is a conscious collaborator in the work of evolution, and a sharer in part of the plans of the Planetary Logos of our scheme. They are given in this brief form both to protect the concealed truths and yet to reveal them to those who are ready.

These seven Words of the solar system, which form the logoic Word which we only know in its triple form as AUM, are revealed at the seven initiations.

At the first initiation is given the Word for the physical plane.

At the second initiation is given the Word for the astral plane.

At the third initiation is given the Word for the lower mental plane.

At this initiation, in which, as earlier said, the Hierophant is the Lord of the World, not only is the Word given for the lower mental plane, but a word which synthesises the three Words for the three worlds is also committed. It is given to the initiate as a topic for meditation, until he takes the fourth initiation, but he is forbidden to use it until the final liberation, as it gives entire control on the three lower planes.

At the fourth initiation the Word for the higher mental plane is imparted.

At the fifth initiation the Word for the buddhic plane is given.

At the sixth initiation the Word for the atmic plane.

At the seventh initiation the Word for the monadic plane is given.

At the sixth initiation the Word which synthesises the fourth, fifth and sixth Words is given by the Hierophant, and thus the initiate wields complete control, through the power of sound, over the substance of the five planes of human evolution. At the seventh initiation the triple AUM, in its true character, is revealed to the illuminated Buddha, and he can then manipulate energy in the six worlds or planes.

Two more initiations can be taken, but little is ever said about them on our earth scheme, for the reason that our scheme is not a "sacred" scheme, and few, if any, of our humanity achieve the eighth and ninth initiations. To do so, they must first pass to another scheme for a lengthy period of service and instruction. All that can be hinted at is, that at the eighth initiation the duality of the triple AUM is brought out, and at the ninth the one sound of the Absolute stands revealed, and its significance is heard and seen. This brings into the consciousness of the initiate somewhat of the energy and power of the *"One about Whom Naught may be Said,"* or the Logos of our Solar Logos. The unit of consciousness is then perfect, as the Logos is perfect, and passes on to work paralleling that of the Solar Logos. Such is the great program and the opportunity reaching out before the sons of man, aye, and before every atom everywhere.

CHAPTER XVI

THE IMPARTING OF THE SECRETS

We now come to the consideration of the secrets committed at the initiation ceremony to the initiate. It is apparent, of course, that only the *fact* of the secret, and an indication as to the matter with which it concerns itself can be touched upon, and even this would be left unmentioned were it not that a knowledge of the general outline of the subject may inspire the applicant for initiation to a more careful study of such a subject and to a more diligent equipping of his mental body with information. Thereby (when in due course of time he stands before the Initiator) he will lose no time in utilising the acquired secret.

The Sevenfold Secret.

After the administration of the oath which pledges the initiate to inviolable secrecy, the newly made initiate advances alone closer to the Hierophant; he then places his hand upon the lower end of the Rod of Initiation which is held in the centre by the Hierophant. The Three Who stand around the throne of office then place Their hands upon the glowing diamond which surmounts the Rod, and when these five personalities are thus linked by the circulating energy emanating from the Rod, the Initiator confides to the initiate the secret. The reason for this is as follows: Each of the five initiations with which we are immediately concerned (for the higher two, not being compulsory, are outside our present consideration) affects one of the five centres in man,

1. The head,
2. The heart,
3. The throat,
4. The solar plexus,
5. The base of the spine,

and reveals to him knowledge concerning the various types of force or energy by which the solar system is animated, and which reach him via a particular etheric centre. At the application of the Rod his centres were affected in a particular fashion. By the impartation of the Secret, the reason is committed to his care, and that reason is demonstrated to him to be identical with that which necessarily produces some particular planetary manifestation, and which causes a certain specific greater cycle.

It might be pointed out that:—

1. Each secret concerns one or other of the seven great planes of the solar system.

2. Each secret deals with, and is the enunciation of, one of the seven laws of nature. They therefore concern one or other of the basic evolutions of each planetary scheme. Each scheme embodies one of the laws as its primary law, and all its evolutions tend to demonstrate the perfection of that law with its six subsidiary mutations, these six differing in one particular in each case according to the primary law manifested.

3. Each secret conveys a key to the *nature* of some particular Planetary Logos, and consequently gives the clue to the characteristics of those Monads who are on that particular planetary ray. It is obvious how necessary such knowledge is to the adept who seeks to work with the sons of men, and to manipulate the force currents affecting them and which they emanate.

4. Each secret concerns some one ray or colour and gives the number, note, and the vibration which corresponds.

These seven secrets are simply short formulas, not of mantric value, such as in the case of the Sacred Word, but of a mathematical nature, precisely worded so as to convey the exact intent of the speaker. To the uninitiated they would look and sound like algebraical formulas, except that each is composed (when seen clairvoyantly) of an oval of a specific hue, according to the secret imparted, containing five peculiar hieroglyphics or symbols. One symbol contains the formula of the law concerned, another gives the planetary key and tone, a third deals with vibration, whilst the fourth shows the number and department under which the ray concerned falls. The last hieroglyph gives one of the seven hierarchical keys by means of which the members of our planetary hierarchy can link up with the solar. This is evidently very vague and ambiguous information, but it will serve to show that, as in the case of the Words, apprehension had to involve two senses, so in the cognition of the secrets the two senses again come into play, and the secret is both heard and appears symbolically to the inner eye.

It will now be apparent why so much stress is laid upon the study of symbols, and why students are urged to ponder and meditate upon the cosmic and systemic signs. It prepares them for the grasp and inner retention of the symbols and formulas which embody the knowledge whereby they can eventually work. These formulas are based upon nine symbols which are now recognised:—

1. The cross in its varying forms.
2. The lotus.
3. The triangle.
4. The cube.

5. The sphere and the point.
6. Eight animal forms, the goat, the bull, the elephant, the man, the dragon, the bear, the lion, and the dog.
7. The line.
8. Certain signs of the Zodiac, hence the need for the study of astrology.
9. The cup, or the holy grail.

All these symbols allied, interwoven, or taken in part, are combined to express one or other of the seven Secrets. The initiate has to recognise them by sight as well as to hear them, and by an effort of the will to imprint them irrevocably upon his memory. This he is aided to do in three ways:—*First,* by a long prior training in observation; this can be begun here and now by all aspirants, and as they learn to imprint details accurately upon their memory they are laying the foundation for that acute instantaneous apprehension of that which is shown them by the Hierophant; *secondly,* by having cultivated within themselves the power to visualise again that which has once been seen. It will be apparent here why the emphasis has been laid by all wise teachers of meditation upon the faculty of the careful building of mental pictures. The aim has been two-fold:—

a. To teach the student to visualise his thought-forms accurately, so that when he begins to create consciously he may lose no time in inaccurate transformation.
b. To enable him to picture again accurately the imparted secret, so that it may instantly be of use to him whenever needed.

Finally, by the strongly applied will of the other four Personalities who are holding the Rod at the same time as the initiate. Their trained intense mental concentration greatly facilitates his apprehension.

In the case of human evolution certain types of force are generated, dealt with, assimilated, and used, at first unconsciously, and finally with full intelligence.

a. In the *Hall of Ignorance* the force or energy of Brahma (the activity and intelligence of substance) is that mostly dealt with, and the man has to learn the meaning of activity based on:—

    a. Inherent energy.
    b. Absorbed energy.
    c. Group energy.
    d. Material energy, or that which is hidden in physical plane matter.

b. In the *Hall of Learning* he becomes aware of, and uses the energy of the second aspect in form building, in social relations, and in family affiliations. He comes to the recognition of sex and its relations, but as yet views this force as something to be controlled, but not consciously and constructively utilised.

c. In the *Hall of Wisdom* he comes to the knowledge of the first aspect of energy, the dynamic use of will in sacrifice, and to him is then committed the key to the threefold mystery of energy. This energy in its threefold aspect he became aware of, in the other two Halls. At the third initiation, and at the fourth and fifth, the three keys to the three mysteries are given to him.

    The key to the mystery sensed in the first Hall, the mystery of Brahma, is handed to him, and he can then unlock the hidden energies of atomic substance.

The key to the mystery of sex, or of the pairs of opposites, is thrust into his hand, and he can then unlock the hidden forces of the will aspect. The dynamo of the solar system is shown to him,—if it might be so expressed—and the intricacies of the mechanism revealed.

The Three Solar Mysteries.

The three mysteries of the solar system are:—

1. *The mystery of Electricity.* The mystery of Brahma. The secret of the third aspect. It is latent in the physical sun.

2. *The mystery of Polarity,* or of the universal sex impulse. The secret of the second aspect. It is latent in the Heart of the Sun, or the subjective Sun.

3. *The mystery of Fire itself,* or the dynamic central systemic force. The secret of the first aspect. It is latent in the Central Spiritual Sun.

Their Sequential Revelation.

The secrets, as imparted sequentially to the initiate, are roughly three in number, though within them may be found lesser mysteries which are earlier revealed. At the third initiation the first of the three fundamental secrets of the solar system is imparted to the initiate, immediately after he has taken the oath. This we might, for lack of a better term, call "the secret of electricity." It concerns the phenomena of the dense objective manifestation of the Logos. It would be wise here for the student to remember that the three planes of the three worlds, physical, astral, and mental, form the dense physical body of the solar Logos, whilst the four higher form His etheric body. Students are apt to forget that our seven planes are the seven sub-planes of the cosmic physical. This has a very definite bearing on the secret of electricity. This is why the secret is not revealed till the third initiation, and is prepared for by the impartation of two lesser secrets which concern the physical and astral planes, and which are imparted at the first two initiations by the Bodhisattva.

Electrical phenomena are scientifically recognised as dual in nature, but the inherent triplicity of electricity is as yet but a matter for speculation for modern science. The fact that it is triple is demonstrated to the initiate at the first initiation, and the secret of how to balance forces on the physical plane, and thereby produce equilibrium, is revealed to him at the first initiation. This secret likewise puts him in touch with certain of the Builders on the physical plane— that is, on the etheric levels—and he can then produce physical plane phenomena should he deem it wise. This he seldom does, as the results gained thereby are practically unimportant and he wastes not energy in this manner. The workers with the involutionary forces, the brothers of darkness, employ this method for the startling and the enthralling of the unwary. Not thus work the brothers of humanity.

The secret of the coherence of the atom is revealed to the initiate, and he then is in a position to study the microcosm under the law of correspondences in a new and illuminating manner. Similarly, through this revelation concerning the densest part of the logoic body, he can ascertain much concerning the previous solar system, and the facts anent the first round of our scheme. This secret is also called "the mystery of matter."

At the second initiation "the secret of the sea" is unfolded to him, and through this revelation two subjects of profound interest become clarified to his inner vision. They are:—

    a. The mystery of the astral light.
    b. The law of karma.

He is, after this, in a position to do two things, without which he cannot work off that which hinders, and thus achieve liberation; he can read the akashic records and ascertain the past, thereby enabling himself to work intelligently in the present, and he can begin to balance his karma, to work off his obligations, and to understand how karma in the three worlds can be negated. The relation of that hierarchy of spiritual beings who are connected with the law of karma as it affects man is demonstrated to him, and he knows with first-hand knowledge that the lords of karma are no myth, or symbolical units, but are highly intelligent entities who wield the law for the benefit of humanity, and thus enable men to become fully self-conscious and self-reliant in the occult sense, and to become creators through perfected knowledge.

At the third initiation "the secret of fohat" is given to him, and then the mystery of the threefold *body* of the triple Logos is his, and the *why* of the phenomena of the dense liquid and gaseous bodies of the Supreme Being is unfolded before his amazed vision. The two secrets previously imparted, and the knowledge which they gave having been utilised, the initiate is now in a position to profit by this greater revelation, and to understand somewhat the following facts:—

    1. The creative process of thought form building.
    2. The transmission of energy from the Ego to the physical body via the force centres on the various planes.

3. The uprising of kundalini, its geometrical progression, and its vivification of all the centres.

By the knowledge thus imparted, and the progress which the initiate has made in the study of the law of analogy, he can comprehend the manipulation of the same forces on a vastly larger scale in the planetary scheme and in the solar system. The method of development in the three earlier rounds is revealed to him, and he understands, practically as well as theoretically, the evolutionary process in its earlier stages. The key to the three lower kingdoms of nature is in his hands, and certain ideas anent the subject of polarity, of at-one-ment, and essential union, are beginning to come within his range of consciousness, only waiting for the fourth initiation to complete the revelation.

This secret of electricity, which is essentially triple in its nature, deals with the Brahma or third aspect, and is called sometimes by the following names:—

1. The Secret of Brahma.
2. The Revelation of the Mother.
3. The Secret of Fohatic Force.
4. The Mystery of the Creator.
5. The Secret of the Three Who issued from the First (solar system),

and also by four mystic phrases conveying much light to the intuition:

6. The Boat of Mystery which Ploughs the Ocean.
7. The Key to the Divine Storehouse.
8. The Light that Guides through the triple caves of Darkness.
9. The Clue to the Energy uniting Fire and Water.

In all these names much information will come to the student who carefully ponders them, remembering that they deal with the Brahma aspect in its lowest manifestation and with the three worlds of human endeavour, and thus meditating, the student must relate this present solar system to the preceding one, in which the Brahma aspect dominated, as the Vishnu, or consciousness aspect dominates in this.

The initiate, through the knowledge imparted, is now in a position to understand his own triple lower nature, and therefore to balance it in relation to the higher, to read the records and understand his place within the group, to manipulate the forces in the three worlds and thereby effect liberation for himself, thus helping the ends of evolution, and to co-operate intelligently with the plans of the Planetary Logos as they may be revealed to him stage by stage. He can now wield power, and becomes a centre of energy in a greatly increased degree, being able to dispense or retract force currents. The moment a man becomes consciously powerful on the mental plane, his power for good is a hundredfold increased.

At the fourth initiation another of the great secrets is revealed to him. It is called "the mystery of polarity," and the clue to the significance of sex in every department of nature on all the planes is given to him. It is not possible to say much along these lines. All that can be done is to enumerate some of the subjects to which it gives the clue, adding to this the information that in our planetary scheme, owing to the point in evolution of our own Planetary Logos, this secret is the most vital. Our Planetary Logos is at the stage wherein He is consciously seeking the at-one-ment with his polar opposite, another Planetary Logos.

The subjects on which this secret throws a flood of light are:—

  a. Sex on the physical plane. It gives us a key to the mystery of the separation of the sexes in Lemurian days.

  b. The balancing of forces in all departments of nature.

  c. The clue as to which Scheme forms with ours a duality.

  d. The true name of our Planetary Logos and His relation to the Solar Logos.

  e. "The Marriage of the Lamb" and the problem of the heavenly bride. A clue to this lies in the solar system of S. . . . which must be read astrologically.

  f. The mystery of the Gemini, and the connection of our particular Planetary Logos with that constellation.

On a lesser scale, and in relation to the microcosm, the following subjects are illuminated when the initiate receives the second great secret, or the fourth which includes the earlier lesser ones:—

  g. The processes of at-one-ment in the different kingdoms of nature. The bridging between the kingdoms is shown him, and he sees the unity of the scheme.

  h. The method of egoic at-one-ment is seen clearly revealed, and the antahkarana is shown in its real nature, and having been thus revealed, is dispensed with.

  i. The essential unity existing between the Ego and the personality is seen.

  j. The relation of the two evolutions, human and deva, is no longer a mystery, but their position in the body of the Heavenly Man is seen to be a fact.

One could go on emphasising the multiplicity of matters which the mystery of polarity, when revealed, makes clear to the initiate, but the above suffices. This secret concerns primarily the Vishnu, or second aspect. It sums up in one short phrase the totality of knowledge gained in the Hall of Wisdom, as the earlier secrets summed up the totality achieved in the Hall of Learning. It deals with consciousness and its development by and through the matter aspect. It concerns literally the unification of the self and the not-self till they are verily and indeed one.

At the fifth initiation the great secret which concerns the fire or spirit aspect is revealed to the wondering and amazed Master, and He realises in a sense incomprehensible to man the fact that all is fire and fire is all. This secret may be said to reveal to the Initiate that which makes clear to Him:—

a. The secret name of the Planetary Logos, thus revealing one syllable of the name of the Solar Logos.
b. The work and method of the destroyer aspect of divinity.
c. The processes whereby obscuration and pralaya are induced.
d. The mathematical formula which sums up all the cycles of manifestation.
e. The triple nature of fire, and the effect of the great fire upon the lesser.

As this Shiva, or first, aspect is the one which will arrive at perfection, or, rather, come within the reach of comprehension within the next solar system, it profits not to continue considering this secret. The following tabulation may make the whole matter clearer to the mind of the student:—

Secret of	Initiation	Logos Concerned	Source of Energy	Planes
Fohat	Third	Brahma Creator	Physical Sun	Seven Six Five
Polarity	Fourth	Vishnu Preserver	Subjective Sun	Four Three
Fire	Fifth	Shiva Destroyer	Central Spiritual Sun	Two

As the student will observe, the source of the particular energy concerned is one aspect of the sun.

At the sixth and seventh initiations two more secrets are revealed, one—a lesser secret—preparing the way for the revelation of the fourth. Only four secrets of a major order are revealed to initiates on this planet, and herein lies the clue to our position in the scheme of solar evolution. There are only five secrets altogether, of a major kind, revealed in this solar system, owing to the fact that this is a system wherein pre-eminently the fifth principle of mind forms the basis of unfoldment. This fifth revelation is only imparted to those who pass to the Schemes of synthesis.

CHAPTER XVII

DIVERSITIES OF INITIATIONS

Major and Minor Initiations.

In dealing with this question of the diversities of initiations it may be of value to the student to remember that the great moment in which a man passed out of the animal kingdom into the human, which is called in many occult textbooks the "moment of individualisation," was in itself one of the greatest of all initiations. Individualisation is the conscious apprehension by the self of its relation to all that constitutes the not-self, and in this great initiatory process, as in all the later ones, the awakening of consciousness is preceded by a period of gradual development; the awakening is instantaneous at the moment of self-realisation for the first time, and is always succeeded by another period of gradual evolution. This period of gradual evolution, in its turn, leads up to a later crisis which is called Initiation. In the one case, we have initiation into self-conscious existence, in the other, initiation into spiritual existence.

These realisations, or apprehended expansions of consciousness, are under natural law, and come in due course of time to every soul *without exception*. In a lesser degree they are undergone daily by every human being, as his mental grip of life and experience gradually grows, but they only become initiations into the wisdom (as differentiated from expansions of knowledge) when the knowledge gained is:—

a. Consciously sought for.
b. Self-sacrificingly applied to life.
c. Willingly used in service for others.
d. Intelligently utilised on the side of evolution.

Only souls of a certain amount of experience and development do all these four things consistently and steadily, and thus transmute knowledge into wisdom, and experience into quality. The ordinary average man transmutes ignorance into knowledge, and experience into faculty. It would be helpful if all of us pondered upon the difference between inherent quality and innate faculty; one is the very nature of buddhi, or wisdom, and the other of manas, or mind. The union of these two, through a man's conscious effort, results in a major initiation.

These results are brought about in two ways:—First, by a man's own unaided effort, which leads him in due course of time to find his own centre of consciousness, to be guided and led by the inner ruler or Ego entirely, and to unravel, through strenuous effort and painful endeavour, the mystery of the universe, which is concealed in material substance energised by Fohat. Secondly, by a man's efforts, supplemented by the intelligent loving co-operation of the Knowers of the race, the Masters of the Wisdom. In this case the process is quicker, for a man comes under instruction—should he so desire—and subsequently, when he has on his part provided the right conditions, there is placed at his disposal the knowledge and the help of Those Who have achieved. In order to avail himself of this help he has to work with the material of his own body, building right material into an ordered form, and has therefore to learn discrimination in the choice of matter, and to understand the laws of vibration and of construction. This entails the mastering, in some measure, of the laws that govern the

Brahma and Vishnu aspects: it means a faculty of vibrating with atomic accuracy, and the development of the quality of attractiveness, which is the basis of the building, or Vishnu aspect.

He has to equip, also, his mental body so that it may be an explainer and transmitter, and not a hindering factor as now. He must likewise develop group activity, and learn to work in a co-ordinated manner with other units. These are the main things that a man must accomplish along the path of initiation, but when he has worked at them, he will find the Way, it will be made clear to him, and he will then join the ranks of the Knowers.

Another point to be remembered is that this effort to make people co-operate intelligently with the Hierarchy, and to train them to join the ranks of the Lodge, is, as earlier pointed out, a special effort (inaugurated in Atlantean days and continued to this time) made by the Hierarchy of the planet, and is very largely in the nature of an experiment. The method whereby a man assumes *conscious* place in the body of a Heavenly Man differs in different planetary Schemes; the Heavenly Man, Who uses our planetary Scheme as His body of manifestation, chooses to work in this particular way during this particular period for His own specific purposes; it is part of the process of vitalising one of His centres, and of linking up His heart centre with its connection in the head. As other of His centres are vitalised, and come into full activity, other methods of stimulating the cells in His body (the deva and human monads) may be followed, but for the present the cosmic Rod of Initiation, which is applied to a Heavenly Man, in much the same manner as the lesser rods are applied to man, is being utilised in such a way that it produces that specific stimulation which demonstrates in the activity of man on the Path of Probation and the Path of Initiation.

Therefore man must recognise the cyclic nature of initiation, and the place of the process in time and space. This is a special period of activity in the cycle of a Heavenly Man, and it works out on our planet as a vast period of trial or initiatory testing; it is, nevertheless, equally a period of vitalisation and of opportunity.

We must also endeavour to realise the fact that initiation may be seen taking place on the three planes in the three worlds, and the thought must ever be borne in mind of the relative value and place of the unit, or cell, in the body of a Heavenly Man. The point must here be emphasised that *the major initiations, or the initiations of manas, are those taken on the mental plane and in the causal body.* They mark the point in evolution where the unit recognises in fact, and not only in theory, his identity with the divine Manasaputra in Whose body he has place. Initiations can be taken on the physical plane, on the astral, and on the lower mental, but they are not considered major initiations, and are not a conscious, co-ordinated, unified stimulation that involves the whole man.

A man, therefore, may take initiation on each plane, but only those initiations which mark his transference from a *lower four into a higher three* are considered so in the real sense of the word, and only those in which a man transfers his consciousness from the lower quarternary into the triad are major initiations. We have, therefore, three grades of initiations:—

First, initiations in which a man transfers his consciousness from the lower four subplanes of the physical, astral, and mental planes respectively, into the higher three subplanes. When this is done upon the mental plane a man is then known technically as a disciple, an initiate, an adept. He uses then each of the three higher subplanes of the mental plane as a point from which to work his way completely out of the three worlds of human manifestation into the triad. Therefore it is apparent that what one might consider as lesser initiations can be taken on the physical and astral planes, in the conscious control of their three higher subplanes. These are true initiations, but do not make a man what is technically understood as a Master of the Wisdom. He is simply an adept of a lesser degree.

Secondly, initiations in which a man transfers his consciousness from plane to plane, instead of from subplane to subplane. Herein comes a point to be carefully recognised. A true Master of the Wisdom has not only taken the lesser initiations referred to above, but has also taken the five steps involved in the conscious control of the five planes of human evolution. It remains for him then to take the two final initiations which make him a Chohan of the sixth degree, and a Buddha, before that control is extended to the remaining two planes of the solar system. It is obvious, therefore, that it is correct to speak of the seven initiations, yet it would be nevertheless equally correct to enumerate five, ten, or twelve initiations. The matter is complicated for occult students, owing to certain mysterious factors about which they can naturally know nothing, and which must remain to them, as yet, utterly incomprehensible. These factors are founded in the individuality of the Heavenly Man Himself, and involve such mysteries as His particular karma, the aim He may have in view for any particular cycle, and the turning of the attention of the cosmic *ego* of a Heavenly Man to His reflection, the evolving Heavenly Man of a solar system.

A further factor may also be found in certain periods of stimulation, and of increased vitalisation, such as a cosmic initiation produces. These outside effects naturally produce results in the units or cells in the body of the Heavenly Man, and lead often to events unforeseen and apparently inexplicable.

Thirdly, initiations in which a Heavenly Man may take either a minor or a major initiation, thereby involving His entire nature. For instance, when individualisation took place during the Lemurian, or the third root race, and the human family in this cycle definitely came into manifestation, it signified a major initiation for our Heavenly Man. The present stimulation in hierarchical effort is leading up to a lesser initiation. Each great cycle sees a major initiation of a Heavenly Man taken on one or other of the globes, and herein again complication lies, and much food for thought.

To the three above points we might also briefly add that of the coming in, or passing out, of any particular ray. The little that can be said upon this point, which is one of the greatest difficulty, might be summed up in the following three statements: First, that initiations taken on the four minor rays rank not in equality with initiations taken upon the major three. This is complicated somewhat by the fact that within the planetary Scheme, during cyclic evolution, a minor ray may be temporarily regarded as a major ray. For instance, at this particular time in our planetary Scheme, the seventh Ray of Ceremonial Law or Order is regarded as a major ray, being a ray of synthesis, and one on which the Mahachohan is blending His work. Secondly, that the first three initiations are taken upon the ray of the Ego, and link a man up with the great White Lodge; the last two are taken upon the ray of the monad, and have a definite effect upon the path for service that will be chosen later by the adept. This statement must be linked up with that earlier made, which stated that the fifth initiation made a man a member of the Greater Lodge, or Brotherhood, on Sirius, being literally the first of the Sirian initiations. The fourth initiation is the synthesis of the Initiations of the Threshold in the Sirian Lodge. Finally, according to the ray on which initiation is taken, so very largely depends the subsequent path of service.

The Day of Opportunity.

The question might here be asked wherein this information is of value to the student. In illustration of this it would be wise if students would ponder the significance of the coming in of the present Ray of Ceremonial Law or Magic. It is the ray that deals with the building forces of nature, that concerns itself with the utilisation of the form intelligently by the life aspect. It is largely the ray of executive work, with the object of building, co-ordinating and producing cohesion in the four lower kingdoms of nature. It is distinguished largely by the energy which manifests itself in ritual, but this word ritual must not be narrowed down to its present use in connection with Masonic, or religious ritual. Its application is far wider than this, and includes the methods of organisation which are demonstrated in all civilised communities, such as in the world of commerce and of finance, and the great business organisations everywhere to be seen. Above all, its interest lies for us in the fact that it is the ray which brings opportunity to the occidental races, and through the medium of this life force of executive organisation, of government by rule and order, by rhythm and by ritual, will come the time wherein the occidental races (with their active, concrete mind, and their vast business capacity) can take initiation,—an initiation, we must remember, upon a ray which is temporarily recognised as a major ray. A large number of the initiates and those who have obtained adeptship in the last cycle, have been orientals and those in Hindu bodies. This cycle has been dominated by the sixth ray, which is just passing out, and the two preceding. In the preservation of equilibrium the time now comes when a period of attainment by occidentals will be seen, and this upon a ray suited to their type of mind. It is interesting to note that the oriental type attains its objective through meditation, with a modicum of executive organisation and ritual, and that the occidental will achieve largely through the organisation which lower mind produces, and a type of meditation of which intense business concentration might be considered an illustration. The one-pointed application of the mind by a European or American business man might be regarded as a type of meditation. In the purification of motive lying back of this application will come, for the occidental, his day of opportunity.

By availing themselves of the present day of opportunity, and by conformity to the rules for treading the Path, will come to many in the West the chance to take these further steps. That opportunity will be found by the man who is ready in the place where he is, and among the familiar circumstances of his daily life. It will be found in attention to duty, in the surmounting of tests and trials, and in that inner adherence to the voice of the God within, which is the mark of every applicant for initiation. Initiation involves the very thing that is done from day to day by any who are consciously endeavouring to train themselves:—the next point to be reached, and the next bit of work to be accomplished is pointed out by the Master (either the God within or a man's Master if he is consciously aware of Him) and the reason is given. Then the Teacher stands aside and watches the aspirant achieve. As He watches, He recognises points of crisis, where the application of a test will do one of two things, focalise and disperse any remaining unconquered evil—if that term might here be used—and demonstrate to the disciple both his weakness and his strength. In the great initiations, the same procedure can be seen, and the ability of the disciple to pass these greater tests and stages is dependent upon his ability to meet and surmount the daily lesser ones. "He that is faithful in that which is least is faithful also in much," is an occult statement of fact, and should characterise the whole daily activity of the true aspirant; the "much" is surmounted and passed, because it is regarded simply as an intensification of the normal, and no initiate has ever passed the great test of initiation who has not accustomed himself to pass lesser tests every day of his life; tests then come to be regarded as normal, and are considered, when encountered, as part of the usual fabric of his life. When this attitude of mind is attained and held, there exists no surprise or possible defeat.

CHAPTER XVIII

THE SEVEN PATHS

As might be expected, very little has appeared in our literature as to the seven Paths which stretch before the man who has reached the fifth initiation. It is obviously impossible, and also unnecessary, to convey to our mind any impression as to the significance of these paths, or as to the attributes needed for their treading. As time progresses and the race reaches a higher point of development, we shall be able to comprehend more, but under the law of economy it would be fruitless effort for the teachers of the race to instruct us on the characteristics needed for the treading of the seven Paths, before we have as yet apprehended or developed those required for traversing the Probationary Path, not to mention the Path of Initiation.

One general fact we do know, and that is, that before these Paths can be trodden, a man must be a Master of the Wisdom, he must be a Brother of Compassion, and he must be able, through intelligence and love, to wield the law. Our part at this time is to fit ourselves for the treading of the Path of Initiation, by the discipline of the Probationary Path, by the careful direction of the life, by obedience to the law as understood, and by service to the race. When we have attained liberation, then these Paths will stretch before us, and the one that we should tread will become apparent to us. All in this system works under the great law of attraction, and therefore, according to our vibration, according to our colour and tone, will depend, in all probability, our choice. The greater free will of the cosmic system is under limitation, just as is the free will of the system of which we are a part, and the free will of man himself. Upon innate quality will depend the direction of our further progress.

These seven Paths might be enumerated as follows, and certain deductions, based on the law of correspondence, might be given out, provided always that we remember that words serve more to blind than to elucidate, and that the briefest details only are possible.

1. *The Path of Earth Service.*

This is the Path that keeps a man linked to the Hierarchy that is pledged to the service of our planet, and to the help of its evolutions. It comprises those who work under the Lord of the World in the seven groups into which our Masters of the Wisdom are divided. Not so many Masters follow this Path as some of the others, and only enough are permitted to do so to carry on planetary evolution satisfactorily. More is known about this path than about the others, and more will be found out as members of our humanity fit themselves to contact the Brotherhood. Their field of employ, Their methods of work, will eventually become exoteric knowledge, and as the seven groups are recognised and known, schools of development for the filling of posts in these groups will be the logical sequence.

2. *The Path of Magnetic Work.*

Those who do the work of wielding forces, or electrical magnetism for the use of the Great Ones on all the planes, pass to this Path. They wield the elemental formative energy, manipulating matter of every density and vibration.

Great waves of ideas and surging currents of public opinion on astral levels, as well as on the higher levels where the Great Ones work, are manipulated by them. A large number of fifth ray people, those who have the Ray of Concrete Knowledge for their monadic ray, pass to this line of endeavour. The inherent quality in the type of the monad settles usually the line of activity. The karma of the fifth ray is one of the factors which produces this. These monads work with Fohat, and must, to the end of the greater manvantara. They have their eventual position on the cosmic mental plane, but as yet the capacity for abstract thought is so little developed that it is impossible for us to comprehend the significance of this expression.

3. The Path of Training for Planetary Logoi.

This Path is trodden by those who will take up the work of the seven Planetary Logoi of the next system, and of the forty-nine sub-planetary Logoi, Their assistants, and of certain other Entities working in that particular department. There will be seven systems, though we are only concerned with the three major systems, of which our present system is the second major system. Each Chohan of a ray takes a certain number of initiates of the sixth initiation and trains them specially for this work; special aptitude in colour and sound predisposes the choice, and the ability to work with "psyche," or the spirits in evolution marks a man out for this high post. We might say that the Planetary Logoi are the divine psychologists, and therefore in the training for this post psychology is the basic subject, though it is a psychology inconceivable as yet to us. Every Planetary Logos has, in His own special planet, schools for the development of subordinate Logoi, and there trains Them for this high office, giving Them opportunity for wide experience. Even the Logoi Themselves progress onward, and Their places must be taken.

4. *The Path to Sirius.*

Very little may be communicated about this Path, and the curiously close relation between it and the Pleiades can only be mentioned, further speculation being impossible. The bulk of liberated humanity goes this way, and the prospect holds out glorious possibilities. The seven stars of the Pleiades are the goal for the seven types, and this is hinted at in the Book of Job, in the words, "Canst thou bind the sweet influence of the Pleiades?" In the mystery of this influence, and in the secret of the sun Sirius, are hidden the facts of our cosmic evolution, and incidentally, therefore, of our solar system.

5. *The Ray Path.*

It is difficult to know by what other name to call this Path, as so little is known about it. In treading it, a man stays on his own ray, and works thereon in the various kingdoms on all the planes, carrying out the behests of the Lord of the World, and working under His direction. It carries a man to every part of the solar system, yet links him definitely with the synthetic ray. It is a very complex path, for it necessitates a capacity for the most intricate mathematics, and an ability to geometrise in a manner incomprehensible to our three-dimensional brains. This path is taken by the man to whom the law of vibration is of profound importance. He works first in the council chamber of the Lord of the World at Shamballa, manipulating the law of vibration on his own ray. Later he will have his habitat on the planet corresponding to his own ray, and not on the earth unless he is on the ray of the Planetary Logos holding sway upon the earth. Later again as his evolution progresses, he will pass to the sun; then having mastered all connected with vibration in this system he will pass to the cosmic system, going off his own ray (which is but a subsidiary ray of one cosmic ray), on to the corresponding cosmic ray.

Just as the evolution of man in this system is fivefold, so in the above we have enumerated the principal five Paths from which a Master has to choose. The remaining two can only be touched upon still more briefly, for they hold but a very few of the evolving sons of men, owing to the high point of attainment necessitated for their entrance, and the fact that those who enter upon them pass out of the system altogether. They do not lead to Sirius, as do some of the other Paths. It will be noted that four groups remain in the system, passing eventually, in dim and distant aeons, to the cosmic planes. One group passes directly to Sirius, and the remaining two groups pass directly after initiation to the cosmic planes, with no period of intermediate work on earth, in the system, or on Sirius. These two Paths are:—

6. *The Path the Logos Himself Is On.*

It will have become apparent to all occult students who have studied with care the world processes in the light of the law of correspondences, that the Logos on the cosmic planes is evolving inner cosmic vision, just as man in his lesser degree is aiming at the same vision in the system. This might be called the development of the cosmic third eye. In the physical plane structure of the eye lies hid the secret and in its study may come some revelation of the mystery.

A certain part of the eye is the nucleus of sight, and the apparatus of vision itself; the remainder of the eye acts as a protecting shell, and both parts are required, and neither can exist without the other. So in this greater case, only the analogy exists on such high levels that words only blur and dim the truth. Certain of the sons of men, a nucleus who reached a very high initiation in the previous solar system, formed an esoteric group around the Logos when He decided upon further progress. In consequence He formed this system, cosmic desire for incarnation driving Him on. This esoteric group remains with the Logos on the atomic, or first plane of the system, on the subjective inner side, and it corresponds, in an occult sense, to the pupil of the eye. The real home of these great Entities is upon the cosmic buddhic plane.

Gradually, by dint of hard effort, certain Masters have qualified Themselves, or are qualifying Themselves, to take the place of the original members of the group, permitting of Their return to a cosmic centre around which our system, and the greater system of Sirius revolve. Only one adept here and there has the necessary qualifications, for it involves the development of a certain type of response to cosmic vibration. It means a specialising in the inner sight, and the development of a certain measure of cosmic vision. More of the deva evolution pass to this path than do the human. Human beings pass to it via the deva evolution, which can be entered by transference to the fifth Path, the ray Path. On this latter Path, the two evolutions can merge, and from the fifth Path the sixth can be entered.

7. *The Path of Absolute Sonship.*

This Sonship is a correspondence on the highest plane to that grade of discipleship which we call "Son of the Master." It is the Sonship to a Being higher than our Logos, of whom we may not speak. It is the great controlling Path of Karma. The Lipika Lords are on this Path, and all who are fitted for that line of work, and who are close to the Logos in a personal intimate sense, pass to the Path of absolute Sonship. It is the Path of the special intimates of the Logos, and into Their hands He has put the working out of karma in the solar system. They know His wishes, His will and His aim, and to Them He entrusts the carrying out of His behests. This group, associated with the Logos, forms a special group linked to a still higher Logos.

CHAPTER XIX

RULES FOR APPLICANTS

There are certain aphorisms and injunctions which the applicant for initiation needs to study and obey. There is a great distinction between the terms "aspirant to the Path" and "applicant for initiation." He who aspires and strives towards discipleship is in no way pledged to the same specific attitude and discipline as is the applicant for initiation, and he can, if he so choose, take as long as he desires in the treading of the Probationary Path. The man who seeks initiation is in a different position, and having once made application has to bring his life under a definite rule, and a strict regime which is only optional to the disciple.

The rules given here are fourteen in number, and are gathered from a series of instructions compiled for those who seek to take the first initiation.

RULES FOR APPLICANTS

Rule I.

Let the disciple search within the heart's deep cave. If there the fire burns bright, warming his brother yet heating not himself, the hour has come for making application to stand before the door.

When love for all beings, irrespective of who they may be, is beginning to be a realised fact in the heart of a disciple, and yet nevertheless love for himself exists not, then comes the indication that he is nearing the Portal of Initiation, and may make the necessary preliminary pledges. These are necessitated before his Master hands in his name as a candidate for initiation. If he cares not for the suffering and pain of the lower self, if it is immaterial to him whether happiness comes his way or not, if the sole purpose of his life is to serve and save the world, and if his brother's need is for him of greater moment than his own, then is the fire of love irradiating his being, and the world can warm itself at his feet. This love has to be a practical, tested manifestation, and not just a theory, nor simply an impractical ideal and a pleasing sentiment. It is something that has grown in the trials and tests of life, so that the primary impulse of the life is towards self-sacrifice and the immolation of the lower nature.

Rule 2.

When application has been made in triple form, then let the disciple withdraw that application, and forget it has been made.

Herein lies one of the initial tests. The disciple's attitude of mind must be that he cares not whether he takes initiation or not. Selfish motive must not enter in. Only those applications which reach the Master through the energy engendered through pure altruistic motive are transmitted by Him to the recording angel of the Hierarchy; only those disciples who seek initiation because of the added power to help and bless that it confers, will find a response to their plea. Those careless of initiation receive not the occult accolade, and those anxious, through selfishness or curiosity, to participate in the mysteries, enter not the door but remain knocking outside. Those who are keen to serve, those who are weighed down with a sense of world need, and the per-

sonal responsibility thereby awakened, and who have fulfilled the law, knock and meet with response, and make
application which meets with recognition. They are the ones
who send forth a cry for added power to aid, which penetrates to the ear of Those Who silently wait.

Rule 3.

Triple the call must be, and long it takes to sound it
forth. Let the disciple sound the cry across the desert,
over the sea, and through the fires which separate him
from the veiled and hidden door.

Under this symbology comes to the disciple the injunction to make the desert of the physical plane life to blossom
like the rose, so that from the garden of the lower life may
arise those sounds and scents, and a vibration strong enough
to cross the intervening space between it and the portal; to
still the restless waters of the emotional life, so that in their
limpid, still expanse, that portal may be reflected, and the
lower life mirror forth the spiritual life of the indwelling
divinity; to pass through the fiery furnace those motives,
words, and thoughts which are the mainspring of activity,
and have their origin upon the mental plane. When these
three aspects of the manifesting Ego, the God within, are
brought under control, co-ordinated, and utilised, then, even
unconsciously to himself, will the voice of the disciple be
heard, demanding the opening of the door. When the lower
life upon the physical plane is fertilised, the emotional stabilised, and the mental transmuted, then naught can prevent the latch upon that door being lifted, and the disciple
passing through. Only synchronous vibration to that which
lies the other side of the door produces its opening, and
when the key of the disciple's life is attuning itself to that

of the hierarchical life, then, one by one, the doors will open, and nothing can keep them closed.

Rule 4.

Let the disciple tend the evolution of the fire; nourish the lesser lives, and thus keep the wheel revolving.

Here comes an injunction to the disciple to remember his responsibility to those many lesser lives which, in their sum-total, compose his triple body of manifestation. Thus is evolution possible, and thus each life, in the different kingdoms of nature, consciously or unconsciously, fulfils its function of rightly energising that which is to it as is the planet to the sun. Thus will the unfolding of the plan logoic proceed with greater accuracy. The kingdom of God is within, and the duty of that inner hidden Ruler is twofold, first, to the lives which form the bodies, physical, astral, and mental, and then to the macrocosm, the world of which the microcosm is but an infinitesimal part.

Rule 5.

Let the applicant see to it that the solar angel dims the light of the lunar angels, remaining the sole luminary in the microcosmic sky.

To fulfil this injunction all applicants need to do two things, first, to study their origin, to realise their own true psychology occultly understood, and to become scientifically aware of the real nature of the Ego, or the Higher Self, functioning in the causal body. Then they have to assert upon the physical plane, through the medium of the three lower bodies, their innate divinity, and to demonstrate in ever increasing degree their essential value. Secondly, to study the constitution of man, to understand the method of functioning in the lower nature, to realise the inter-dependence and interrelation of all living things, and thus bring the lesser lives, which compose those three bodies of manifestation, under control. Thus the solar Lord, the inner Reality, the Son of the Father, and the Thinker on his own plane becomes the intermediary between that which is of the earth, earthy, and that which finds its home within the sun. Two verses in the Christian Bible hide something of this idea within themselves, and students in the occident may find it helpful to meditate upon them:—"The kingdoms of this world are become the kingdom of our Lord and of His Christ." "O Lord, our God, other lords beside Thee have had dominion over us, but by Thee only will we make mention of Thy name." The last verse is particularly interesting, as it demonstrates the suppression of the lower sound and creative force by that which is of higher origin.

Rule 6.

The purificatory fires burn dim and low when the third is sacrificed to the fourth. Therefore let the disciple refrain from taking life, and let him nourish that which is lowest with the produce of the second.

This rule might be summed up in the trite instruction to each disciple that he be strictly vegetarian. The lower nature becomes clogged and heavy, and the inner blaze cannot shine forth when meat is included in the diet. This is a drastic rule for applicants, and may not be violated. Aspirants can choose to eat meat or not as they prefer, but at a certain stage upon the path it is essential that all meat eating of every kind be stopped, and the strictest attention must be paid to diet. A disciple must confine himself to vegetables, grains, fruits and nuts. Only thus can he build the type of physical body which can stand the entry of the real man who has stood in his subtler bodies before the Initiator. Should he not do this, and should it be possible for him to take initiation without having thus prepared himself, the physical body would be shattered by the energy pouring through the newly stimulated centres, and dire danger to the brain, the spine, or the heart would eventuate.

It must, of course, here be recognised that no hard or fast rules can ever be laid down, except the initial one that for all applicants for initiation meat, fish, and fermented liquors of all kinds, as well as the use of tobacco, are absolutely forbidden. For those who can stand it, eggs and cheese are sometimes better eliminated from the diet, but this is not in any way compulsory. It is advisable always that those who are in process of developing psychic faculties of any kind should not permit themselves to eat eggs and very little cheese. Milk and butter come under a different category, and most initiates and applicants find it necessary to retain them in the diet. A few exceptional people can subsist and retain their full physical energies on the diet mentioned in the preceding paragraph, but there the ideal is embodied, and, as we all know, the ideal is seldom attainable in the present transitional period.

In this connection two things should be emphasised:— First, the need that all applicants have for common sense; this factor is very often lacking, and students do well to remember that unbalanced fanatics are not desirable members of the Hierarchy. Equilibrium, a just sense of proportion, a due regard for environing conditions, and a sane common sense are the marks of the true occultist. When a real sense of humour exists likewise, many dangers will be avoided. Secondly, a recognition of *time*, and an ability to move slowly when effecting changes in the diet and in the habits of a lifetime. Everything in nature progresses slowly, and applicants must learn the occult truth of the words:—"Make haste slowly." A process of gradual elimination is usually the path of wisdom, and this eliminating period should—under ideal conditions which so seldom exist —cover the stage which we call that of the aspirant, so that when a man becomes an applicant for initiation he will have done the necessary preparatory purification of the diet.

Rule 7.

Let the disciple turn his attention to the enunciating of those sounds which echo in the halls where walks the Master. Let him not sound the lesser notes which awaken vibration within the halls of Maya.

The disciple who seeks to enter within the Portals of Initiation cannot do so until he has learnt the power of speech and the power of silence. This has a deeper and a wider significance than perhaps is apparent, for it holds, if rightly interpreted, the key to manifestation, the clue to the great cycles, and the revelation of the purpose underlying pralaya. Until a man comprehends the significance of the spoken word, and until he utilises the silence of the high places for the bringing about of desired effects on one plane or another, he cannot be admitted into those realms wherein every sound and every word spoken produces powerful results in matter of some kind, being energised by two predominant factors, (a) a powerful will, scientifically applied, (b) right motive, purified in the fires.

An adept is a creator in mental matter, an originator of impulses on the mental plane, thereby producing results in astral or physical manifestation. These results are powerful and effective, and hence the necessity for their originator to be pure in thought, accurate in word, and skilful in action. When these ideas are realised by applicants, the immediate consequence will be important changes in the life of every day. These changes might, for the sake of their practical use, be enumerated as follows:

a. Motives will be closely searched, and a strict check will be kept upon originating impulses. Hence during the first year in which the applicant devotes him-self to the work of preparation for initiation he will, three times a day, keep a written account of the investigations he pursues, which concern his motives, or the mainspring of action.

b. Speech will be watched, and an endeavour will be made to eliminate all unkind, unnecessary and waste-ful words. The effects of the spoken word will be studied, and be traced back to those originating im-pulses which, in every case, initiate action upon the physical plane.

c. Silence will be cultivated, and applicants will be care-ful to preserve strict silence concerning themselves, their occult work or knowledge, the affairs of those associated with them, and the work of their occult group. Only in group circles or in connection with their superiors will a wise latitude in speech be per-mitted. There is a time to speak. That time comes when the group can be served by wise words, a careful intimation of conditions, good or bad, and a rare, but necessary word to some brother concern-ing the inner life, or to some superior or group of officials, in cases where a brother may be hindering a group through error of some kind, or might help the group if put to different work.

d. The effect of the Sacred Word will be studied, and conditions for its use wisely arranged. The sounding of the Word, and its effect upon a particular esoteric centre (not in any case whatsoever a physical centre) will be watched, and the life thereby influenced and regulated.

The whole question of the study of sound and of words, sacred or otherwise, has to be taken up by applicants for initiation. This is something which must be faced more strenuously by all eventuating occult groups.

Rule 8.

When the disciple nears the portal, the Greater Seven must awaken and bring forth response from the lesser seven upon the double circle.

This rule is a very difficult one, and one which holds in it the elements of danger for the man who undertakes too early to tread the final path. Literally it can be interpreted thus: The would-be initiate must develop somewhat the vibration of the seven head centres, and thus sweep into increased vibratory activity the seven centres in the body upon the etheric plane; affecting also, through reciprocal vibration, the seven physical centres which are inevitably stimulated when the etheric centres approach their maximum vibration. It is not necessary to enlarge upon this point beyond pointing out that as the seven centres within the head become responsive to the Ego the following seven centres,

1. The head, considered as a unit,
2. The heart,
3. The throat,
4. The solar plexus,
5. The base of the spine,

6. The spleen,
7. The organs of generation,

arc also affected, but affected along the line of purification and control. This will produce results in the definitely physical organs through which man functions on the physical plane. In illustration:—Man can then transfer consciously the creative fire and energy from the organs of generation to the throat, or, through the conscious control of the heart, produce suspended animation of the physical body. This is not achieved through what is called Hatha Yoga practices, or concentrating the attention upon the physical organs, but through the development of the control by the inner God, Who works through the head centre and thus dominates all else.

The applicant, therefore, will bend all his energies towards the development of the spiritual life, which development will be the outcome of right thinking, meditation, and service. Through deep study of all there is to be known concerning energy and its focal points, he will co-ordinate his life so that the life of the spirit may flow through it. This study can only be safely undertaken at present in group work and under guidance from a teacher; the pupils will pledge themselves to permit no experimentation in their lives, and no careless trifling with the fires of the body. They will simply apply themselves to a theoretical comprehension and a life of service.

The centres will then develop normally, whilst the applicant bends his attention to loving his brother perfectly in truth and in deed, to serving wholeheartedly, to thinking intelligently, and to keeping a close watch upon himself. He will also record all that seems to him in his inner life to be concerned with the evolution of the centres. This record can be surveyed by the teacher, comment made, deduction sought, and the quota of information thus gained filed for group reference. In this way much knowledge can be stored up for use.

The applicant who misuses knowledge, who indulges in such practices as "breathing for development," or concentrating upon the centres, will inevitably fail in his endeavour to reach the portal, and will pay the price in his body by the appearance of insanity, of neurasthenic conditions, and various physical ills.

Rule 9.

Let the disciple merge himself within the circle of his other selves. Let but one colour blend them and their unity appear. Only when the group is known and sensed can energy be wisely emanated.

One thing all disciples and applicants for initiation have to do is to find that particular group of servers to which they belong on the inner plane, to recognise them upon the physical plane, and to unite with them in service for the race. This recognition will be based upon:—

a. Unity of aim.
b. Oneness of vibration.
c. Identity in group affiliation.
d. Karmic links of long standing.
e. Ability to work in harmonious relation.

Superficially, this may appear one of the easiest of the rules, but in practice it is not so. Mistakes are easily made, and the problem of working harmoniously in group alignment is not so simple as it may appear. Egoic vibration and relationship may exist, yet the outer personalities may not harmonise. It is the work, then, of the applicant to strengthen the grip of his Ego upon his personality, so that the esoteric group relation may become possible upon the physical plane. He will do this by the disciplining of his own personality, and not by the correction of his brothers.

Rule 10.

The Army of the Voice, the devas in their serried ranks, work ceaselessly. Let the disciple apply himself to the consideration of their methods; let him learn the rules whereby that Army works within the veils of Maya.

This rule refers to the work of occult investigation, which must be pursued at some time or another by all who seek initiation. Though it is not safe for the uninitiated to tamper with the parallel evolution of the devas, yet it is necessary and safe to investigate the procedure pursued by the builders, the methods followed by them, in reproducing from the archetype, via the etheric that which we call physical manifestation; their groups must be somewhat theoretically cognised, and the sounds whereby they are swept into activity considered. This involves, therefore, the organised study, by all applicants, of:—

1. The purpose of sound.
2. The esoteric meaning of words, of grammar, and of syntax.
3. The laws of vibration and of electricity, and many other subsidiary studies which concern themselves with the manifestation of divinity and consciousness through the medium of deva substance and the activity of the controlling devas. The laws of the macrocosm will be investigated, and the correspondence between the activities of the microcosm, and the active manifestation of the macrocosm will be recognised.

Rule 11.

Let the disciple transfer the fire from the lower triangle to the higher, and preserve that which is created through the fire of the midway point.

This means, literally, the control by the initiate of the sex impulse, as usually understood, and the transference of the fire which now normally vitalises the generative organs to the throat centre, thus leading to creation upon the mental plane through the agency of mind. That which is to be created must then be nourished and sustained by the love energy of nature issuing from the heart centre.

The lower triangle referred to is:—

1. The solar plexus.
2. The base of the spine.
3. The generative organs.

Whilst the higher one is, as pointed out:—

1. The head.
2. The throat.
3. The heart.

This might be interpreted by the superficial reader as an injunction to the celibate life, and the pledging of the applicant to abstain from all physical manifestation of the sex impulse. This is not so. Many initiates have attained their objective when duly and wisely participating in the marriage relation. An initiate cultivates a peculiar attitude of mind, wherein there is a recognition that all forms of manifestation are divine, and that the physical plane is as much a form of divine expression as any of the higher planes. He realises that the lowest manifestation of divinity must be under the conscious control of that indwelling divinity, and that all acts of every kind should be regulated by the endeavour to fulfil every duty and obligation, to control every action and deed, and to utilise the physical vehicle so that the group may be thereby benefited and aided in its spiritual progress, and the law perfectly fulfilled.

That it may be advisable, at certain stages, for a man to perfect control along any particular line through a temporary abstention is not to be denied, but that is a means to an end, and will be succeeded by stages when—the control having been gained—the man demonstrates perfectly through the medium of the physical body, the attributes of divinity, and every centre will be normally and wisely used, and thus race purposes furthered.

Initiates and Masters, in many cases marry, and normally perform their duties as husbands, wives, and householders, but all is controlled and regulated by purpose and intention, and none is carried away by passion or desire. In the perfect man upon the physical plane, all the centres are under complete control, and their energy is legitimately used; the spiritual will of the divine inner God is the main factor, and there will be a unity of effort shown on all the planes through all the centres for the greatest good of the greatest number.

This point has been touched upon because so many students go astray upon these matters, and cultivate either an attitude of mind which results in the complete atrophying of the entire normal physical nature, or indulge in an orgy of license under the specious plea of "stimulating the centres," and thus furthering astral development. The true initiate should be known by his wise and sanctified normality, by his steady conformity to that which is best for the group as emphasised by the group laws of the land, by his control and his refraining from excess of any kind, and by the example he sets to his environing associates of spiritual living and moral rectitude, coupled with the discipline of his life.

Rule 12.

Let the disciple learn the use of the hand in service; let him seek the mark of the messenger in his feet, and let him learn to see with the eye that looks out from between the two.

This rule looks easy of interpretation upon the first reading, and seems to enjoin upon the applicant the use of the hands in service, of the feet upon hierarchical errands, and the development of clairvoyance. But the real meaning is much more esoteric. Occultly understood, the "use of the hands" is the utilisation of the chakras (or centres) in the palms of the hands in:—

a. Healing bodily ills.
b. Blessing, and thus curing emotional ills.
c. Raised in prayer, or the use of the centres of the hands during meditation in the manipulation of mental matter and currents.

These three points will bear careful consideration, and much may be learnt by occidental students from the study of the life of Christ, and a consideration of His methods in using His hands. More cannot be said here, as the subject is too vast to be enlarged upon in this brief commentary.

The "mark of the messenger" in the feet, is a reference to that well-known symbol of the wings on the heels of Mercury. Much upon this subject will be revealed to students in occult schools who will gather together all that can be found concerning the Messenger of the Gods, and who also will study with care information which astrological students have gleaned anent the planet Mercury, and which occult students have gathered concerning the inner round.

On the surface, the expression "the eye which looks out from between the two" seems to signify the third eye, which clairvoyants utilise, but the meaning is very much deeper than that, and lies hidden in the following facts:—

a That the inner vision is that which all self-conscious beings, from a Logos to a man, are in process of developing.

b. That the Ego, or Higher Self, is literally to the Monad what the third eye is to man, and therefore is described as looking out from between the Monad or spiritual self on the one hand, and the personal self on the other.

In the fullest sense, therefore, this rule incites the applicant to develop self-consciousness, and thus learn to function in the causal body on the higher levels of the mental plane, controlling from thence all the lower vehicles and seeing clearly all that can be seen in the three worlds, in the past and in the future.

Rule 13.

Four things the disciple must learn and comprehend before he can be shewn that inmost mystery: first, the laws of that which radiates; the five meanings of magnetisation make the second; the third is transmutation, or the secret lost of alchemy; and lastly the first letter of the Word which has been imparted, or the hidden name egoic.

This rule cannot be enlarged upon. It concerns mysteries and subjects too immense to be fully handled here. It is

included in these rules so that it may form a subject for meditation, for study, and for group discussion.

The final rule is very brief and consists of five words:

Rule 14.
   Listen, touch, see, apply, know.

These words concern what the Christian might aptly call
the consecration of the three major senses, and their utilisation in the evolution of the inner spiritual life, application
then made of that which is learnt and ascertained, followed
by the fruition of realised knowledge.

AN ESOTERIC CATECHISM

The following are some words from Archive XIII of the Masters' Records, that carry with them a message for the struggler on the Way. They are somewhat on the line of an old catechism, and used to be recited by the participants in the lesser mysteries before they passed on into the greater.

What seest thou, O Pilgrim? Lift up thine eyes and tell what thou beholdest.

I see a ladder, mounting within the vault of blue, its feet lost sight of in the mists and fogs that circle round our planet.

Where standest thou, O Pilgrim? On what are placed thy feet?

I stand upon a portion of the ladder, the fourth division well nigh mounted; its latter part stretches before me into the darkness of a stormy night. Beyond that sphere of utter gloom I see the ladder rise again, radiant and glowing in its fifth division.

What marks those portions which you thus describe as separated from another part? Do not all form but one completed ladder of clearly marked proportions?

Always a gap appeareth to the eye, which (when approached more closely) resolveth then itself into a Cross, by which one mounteth to the next division.

What causeth then the Cross? How mount you by its aid?

The Cross is formed by aspirations, instilled by Godlike urge, which cut athwart the lower world desires, implanted by the life developed from below.

Explain more clearly what you mean, and how that Cross becomes the Way.

The arms that form the Cross become the great dividing line, placed twixt the lower and the higher. Upon those arms the hands are nailed,—the hands that grasp and hold, ministering to the lower needs, trained thus through many aeons. Lo, when the hands are helpless held, and cannot grasp and hold, the inner life slips from its sheath, mounting the limb upright. It passeth from the lower fourth, and the Cross doth bridge the gap.

Pass they with ease that mount that limb, and leave the fourth behind?

They pass through tears, through clouds and mists; they suffer and they die. They bid adieu to all earth's friends; they mount the Way alone; they bridge the gap with loving deeds done in the pain of living; they lift one hand aloft to Him Who standeth just above; they lean one downward to the man who standeth next below. The hands, freed from the transverse arms, are freed but to be held. Only the empty nail-marked hands can keep the chain complete.

Where ends the ladder's length? What point of gloom is pierced by it and where projects its end?

It cuts the crystallising sphere with all its myriad forms; it pierces through the watery plane, washed by the swirling tides; it passes through the nethermost hell, down into densest maya, and ends within the latent fire, the molten lake of fiercest burning, touching the denizens of fire, the Agnichaitans of the scarlet heat.

Where mounts the ladder's length? Where is its consummation?

It mounteth through the radiant spheres, through all their six divisions. It riseth to the mighty Seat within the final fifth, and passeth from that mighty Seat to yet another greater.

Who sits upon that mighty Seat within the final fifth?

He with the Name we mention not, save in utter adoration; the Youth of Endless Summers, the Light of Life itself, the Wondrous One, the Ancient One, Lord of Venusian Love, the great Kumara with the Flaming Sword, the Peace of all the Earth.

Sits He alone, this Wondrous One, upon His sapphire throne?

He sits alone, yet close upon the rainbow steps there stand three other Lords, garnering the product of Their work and sacrificing all Their gain to aid the Lord of Love.

Are They assisted in Their work? Do other Ones of greater powers than ours stand too upon the ladder?

These mighty Four, Action and Love, in wise co-operation work with Their Brothers of a lesser grade, the three Great Lords we know.

Who aid these mighty Lords? Who carry on Their work, linking the lower with the higher?

The Brothers of Logoic Love in all Their many grades. They stay within the final fifth till it absorbeth all the fourth.

Where mounts the ladder then?

To the greatest Lord of all, before Whom e'en that Ancient One bends in obeisance low; before Whose throne of effulgent light Angels of highest rank, Masters and Lords of uttermost compassion, prostrate Themselves and humbly bend, waiting the *Word* to rise.

When sounds that *Word* and what transpires when it echoes through the spheres?

That *Word* sounds not till all is done, until the Lord of endless love deemeth the work correct. He uttereth then a lesser Word that vibrateth through the scheme. The greater Lord of cosmic Love, hearing the circling sound, addeth completion to the chord, and breatheth forth the whole.

What will be seen, O Pilgrim on the Way, when sounds that final chord?

The music of the endless spheres, the merging of the seven; the end of tears, of sin, of strife, the shattering of forms; the finish of the ladder, the blending in the All, completion of the circling spheres and their entry into peace.

What part, O Pilgrim on the Way, play you within this scheme? How will you enter into peace? How stand before your Lord?

I play my part with stern resolve, with earnest aspiration;

I look above, I help below; I dream not, nor I rest; I toil; I serve; I reap; I pray; I am the Cross; I am the Way; I tread upon the work I do; I mount upon my slain self; I kill desire, and I strive, forgetting all reward. I forego peace; I forfeit rest, and in the stress of pain I lose myself and find Myself and enter into peace.

THE GREAT INVOCATION

From the point of Light within the Mind of God
  Let light stream forth into the minds of men.
    Let Light descend on Earth.

From the point of Love within the Heart of God
  Let love stream forth into the hearts of men.
    May Christ return to Earth.

From the centre where the Will of God is known
  Let purpose guide the little wills of men—
    The purpose which the Masters know and serve.

From the centre which we call the race of men
  Let the Plan of Love and Light work out
    And may it seal the door where evil dwells.

Let Light and Love and Power restore the Plan on Earth.

"The above Invocation or Prayer does not belong to any person or group but to all Humanity. The beauty and the strength of this Invocation lies in its simplicity, and in its expression of certain central truths which all men, innately and normally, accept—the truth of the existence of a basic Intelligence to Whom we vaguely give the name of God; the truth that behind all outer seeming, the motivating power of the universe is Love; the truth that a great Individuality came to earth, called by Christians, the Christ, and embodied that love so that we could understand; the truth that both love and intelligence are effects of what is called the Will of God; and finally the self-evident truth that only through *humanity* itself can the Divine Plan work out."—ALICE A. BAILEY.

GLOSSARY

Adept. A Master, or human being who, having traversed the path of evolution and entered upon the final stage of the path, the Path of Initiation, has taken five of the Initiations, and has therefore passed into the Fifth, or Spiritual kingdom, having but two more Initiations to take.

Adi. The First; the primeval; the atomic plane of the solar system; the highest of the seven planes.

Agni. The Lord of Fire in the Vedas. The oldest and most revered of the Gods in India. One of the three great deities Agni, Vayu and Surya, and also all the three, as he is the triple aspect of fire; fire is the essence of the solar system. The Bible says: "Our God is a consuming fire." It is also the symbol of the mental plane of which Agni is paramountly lord.

Agnichaitans. A group of fire devas.

Atlantis. The continent that was submerged in the Atlantic ocean, according to the occult teaching and Plato. Atlantis was the home of the Fourth Root Race, whom we now call the Atlanteans.

Antahkarana. The path, or bridge, between higher and lower mind, serving as a medium of communication between the two. It is built by the aspirant himself in mental matter.

Ashram. The centre to which the Master gathers the disciples and aspirants for personal instruction.

Atma. The Universal Spirit; the divine Monad; the seventh Principle; so called in the septenary constitution of man. (See diagram in Introduction.)

Atomic subplane. The matter of the solar system is divided by the ocultists into seven planes or states, the highest of which is the atomic plane. Similarly, each of the seven planes is divided into seven subplanes, of which the highest is called the atomic subplane. There are therefore forty-nine subplanes, and seven of these are atomic.

Aura. A subtle invisible essence or fluid which emanates from human and animal bodies, and even from things. It is a psychic effluvium, partaking of both mind and body. It is electro-vital, and also electro-mental.

Auric egg. An appellation that has been given to the causal body owing to its form.

Bodhisattva. Literally, he whose consciousness has become intelligence, or buddhi. Those who need but one more incarnation to become perfect buddhas. As used in these letters the Bodhisattva is the name of the office which is at present occupied by the Lord Maitreya, Who is known in the occident as the Christ. This office might be translated as that of World Teacher. The Bodhisattva is the Head of all the religions of the world, and the Master of the Masters and of the angels.

Buddha (The). The name given to Gautama. Born in India about B.C. 621 he became a full buddha in B.C. 592. The Buddha is one who is the "Enlightened," and has attained the highest degree of knowledge possible for man in this solar system.

Buddhi. The Universal Soul or Mind. It is the spiritual soul in man (the Sixth Principle) and therefore the vehicle of Atma, the Spirit, which is the Seventh Principle.

Causal Body. This body is, from the standpoint of the physical plane, no body, either subjective or objective. It is, nevertheless, the centre of the egoic consciousness, and is formed of the conjunction of buddhi and manas. It is relatively permanent and lasts throughout the long cycle of incarnations, and is only dissipated after the fourth initiation, when the need for further rebirth on the part of a human being no longer exists.

Chohan. Lord, Master, a Chief. In this book it refers to those Adepts who have gone on and taken the sixth initiation.

Deva (or Angel). A god. In Sanskrit a resplendent deity. A Deva is a celestial being, whether good, bad, or indifferent. Devas are divided into many groups, and are called not only angels and archangels, but lesser and greater builders.

Egoic Groups. On the third subplane of the fifth plane, the mental, are found the causal bodies of the individual men and women. These bodies, which are the expression of the Ego, or of the individualised self-consciousness, are gathered together into groups according to the ray or quality of the particular Ego involved.

Elementals. The Spirits of the Elements; the creatures involved in the four kingdoms, or elements, Earth, Air, Fire, and Water. Except a few of the higher kinds and their rulers they are forces of nature more than ethereal men and women.

Etheric body. (Etheric double.) The physical body of a human being is, according to occult teaching, formed of two parts, the dense physical body, and the etheric body. The dense physical body is formed of matter of the lowest three subplanes of the physical plane. The etheric body is formed of the four highest or etheric subplanes of the physical plane.

Fifth Principle. The principle of mind; that faculty in man which is the intelligent thinking principle, and which differentiates man from the animals.

Fohat. Cosmic electricity; primordial light; the ever-present electrical energy; the universal propelling vital force; the ceaseless destructive and formative power; the synthesis of the many forms of electrical phenomena.

Guru. Spiritual Teacher. A Master in metaphysical and ethical doctrines.

Hierarchy. That group of spiritual beings on the inner planes of the solar system who are the intelligent forces of nature, and who control the evolutionary processes. They are themselves divided into twelve Hierarchies. Within our planetary scheme, the earth scheme, there is a reflection of this Hierarchy which is called by the occultist the Occult Hierarchy. This Hierarchy is formed of chohans, adepts, and initiates working through their disciples, and, by this means, in the world. (See diagram page 48.)

Initiations. From the Latin root meaning the first principles of any science. Process of penetrating into the mysteries of the science of the Self and of the one self in all selves. The Path of Initiation is the final stage of

the path of evolution trodden by man, and is divided
into five stages, called the Five Initiations.

Jiva. A separated unit of consciousness.

Kali yuga. "Yuga" is an age or cycle. According to the
Indian philosophy our evolution is divided into four
yugas or cycles. The Kali-yuga is the present age. It
means the "Black Age," a period of 432,000 years.

Karma. Physical action. Metaphysically, the law of retribution; the law of cause and effect, or ethical causation.
There is the karma of merit and the karma of demerit.
It is the power that controls all things, the resultant of
moral action, or the moral effect of an act committed for
the attainment of something which gratifies a personal
desire.

Kumaras. The highest seven self-conscious beings in the
solar system. These seven Kumaras manifest through the
medium of a planetary scheme in the same way as a
human being manifests through the medium of a physical
body. They are called by the Hindu "the mind-born
sons of Brahma" amongst other names. They are the
sumtotal of intelligence and of wisdom. Within the
planetary scheme the reflection of the systemic order
is also seen. At the head of our world evolution stands
the first Kumara, aided by six other Kumaras, three
exoteric and three esoteric, Who are the focal points
for the distribution of the force of the systemic Kumaras.

Kundalini. The power of Life: one of the forces of nature.
It is a power known only to those who practise concentration in yoga, and is centred within the spine.

Lemuria. A modern term first used by some naturalists and
now adopted by Theosophists to indicate a continent

that, according to the Secret Doctrine of the East, preceded Atlantis. It was the home of the third root race.

Logos. The deity manifested through every nation and people. The outward expression, or the effect of the cause which is ever concealed. Thus, speech is the Logos of thought, hence it is aptly translated by the "verbum" and the "word" in its metaphysical sense. (See John 1:1-3.)

Lord of Civilisation. (See Mahachohan.)

Lords of the Flame. One of the great Hierarchies of spiritual beings who guide the solar system. They took control of the evolution of humanity upon this planet about 18 million years ago, during the middle of the Lemurian, or third root race.

Macrocosm. The great universe, literally; or God manifesting through His body, the solar system.

Mahachohan. The Head of the third great department of the Hierarchy. This great being is the Lord of Civilisation, and the flowering forth of the principle of intelligence. He is the embodiment on the planet of the third, or intelligence aspect of deity in its five activities.

Mahamanvantara. The great interludes of time between two solar systems. This term is frequently applied to the greater solar cycles. It implies a period of universal activity.

Manas, or Manasic Principle. Literally, the Mind, the mental faculty; that which distinguishes man from the mere animal. It is the individualising principle; that which enables man to know that he exists, feels, and knows. It is divided in some schools into two parts, higher or abstract mind, and lower or concrete mind.

Mantrams. Verses from the Vedas. In the exoteric sense a mantram (or that psychic faculty or power that conveys perception or thought) is the older portion of the Vedas, the second part of which is composed of the Brahmanas. In esoteric phraseology mantram is the word made flesh, or rendered objective through divine magic. A form of words or syllables rhythmically arranged, so that when sounded certain vibrations are generated.

Manu. The representative name of the great Being Who is the Ruler, primal progenitor and chief of the human race. It comes from the Sanskrit root "man"—to think.

Manvantara. A period of activity as opposed to a period of rest, without reference to any specific length of cycle. Frequently used to express a period of planetary activity and its seven races.

Maya. Sanskrit, "Illusion." Of the principle of form or limitation. The result of manifestation. Generally used in a relative sense for phenomena or objective appearances that are created by the mind.

Mayavi Rupa. Sanskrit, "Illusive Form." It is the body of manifestation created by the adept by an act of will for use in the three worlds. It has no material connection with the physical body. It is spiritual and ethereal and passes everywhere without let or hindrance. It is built by the power of the lower mind, of the highest type of astral matter.

Microcosm. The little universe, or man manifesting through his body, the physical body.

Monad. The One. The threefold spirit on its own plane. In occultism it often means the unified triad—Atma, Buddhi, Manas; Spiritual Will, Intuition and Higher

mind,—or the immortal part of man which reincarnates
in the lower kingdoms and gradually progresses through
them to man and thence to the final goal.

Nirmanakaya. Those perfected beings who renounce Nir-
vana (the highest state of spiritual bliss) and choose a
life of self-sacrifice, becoming members of that invisible
host which ever protects humanity within karmic limits.

Permanent atom. Those five atoms, with the mental unit,
one on each of the five planes of human evolution (the
mental unit being also on the mental plane) which the
monad appropriates for purposes of manifestation. They
form a stable centre and are relatively permanent.
Around them the various sheaths or bodies are built.
They are literally small force centres.

Planetary Logos. This term is generally applied to the seven
highest spirits corresponding to the seven archangels of
the Christian. They have all passed through the human
stage and are now manifesting through a planet and its
evolutions, in the same way that man manifests through
his physical body. The highest planetary spirit working
through any particular globe is, in reality, the personal
God of the planet.

Prakriti. Derives its name from its function as the material
cause of the first evolution of the universe. It may be
said to be composed of two roots, "pra" to manifest,
and "krita" to make; meaning, that which caused the
universe to manifest itself.

Prana. The Life Principle, the breath of Life. The occultist believes the following statement: "Life we look
upon as the one form of existence, manifesting in what
is called matter, or what, incorrectly separating them,

we name Spirit, Soul, and Matter in man. Matter is the vehicle for the manifestation of soul on this plane of existence; soul is the vehicle for the manifestation of spirit, and these three as a trinity are synthesised by Life, which pervades them all."

Purusha. The spiritual self. The embodied self. The word literally means "The dweller in the city"—that is, in the body. It is derived from the Sanskrit "pura" which means city or body, and "usha" a derivative of the verb "vas," to dwell.

Quaternary. The fourfold lower self, or man, in the three worlds. There are various divisions of this, but perhaps for our purpose the best is to enumerate the four as follows:

1. Lower mind.
2. Emotional or kamic body.
3. Prana, or the Life Principle.
4. The etheric body, or the highest division of the twofold physical body.

Raja Lord. The word "Raja" simply means King or Prince; the word has been applied to those great angels or entities who ensoul the seven planes. These are great devas who are the sumtotal and the controlling intelligence of a plane.

Raja Yoga. The true system of developing psychic and spiritual powers and union with one's higher self or the Ego. It involves the exercise, regulation, and concentration of thought.

Ray. One of the seven streams of force of the Logos; the seven great lights. Each of them is the embodiment of a great cosmic entity. The seven Rays can be divided into the three Rays of Aspect and the four Rays of Attribute, as follows:

Rays of Aspect

1. The Ray of Will, or Power.
2. The Ray of Love-Wisdom.
3. The Ray of Activity or Adaptability.

Rays of Attribute

4. The Ray of Harmony, Beauty, Art, or Unity.
5. The Ray of Concrete Knowledge or Science.
6. The Ray of Abstract Idealism or Devotion.
7. The Ray of Ceremonial Magic, or Law.

The above names are simply some chosen from among many, and embody the different aspects of force by means of which the Logos manifests.

Ring-pass-not. This is at the circumference of the manifested solar system, and is the periphery of the influence of the sun, both esoterically and exoterically understood. The limit of the field of activity of the central life force.

Root Race. One of the seven races of man which evolve upon a planet during the great cycle of planetary existence. This cycle is called a world period. The Aryan root race, to which the Hindu, European, and modern American races belong, is the fifth, the Chinese and Japanese belonging to the fourth race.

Sensa, or Senzar. The name for the secret sacerdotal language, or the "mystery speech" of the initiated adepts all over the world. It is a universal language, and largely a hieroglyphic cypher.

Shamballa. The City of the Gods, which is in the West to some nations, in the East to others, in the North or South to yet others. It is the sacred island in the Gobi Desert. It is the home of mysticism and the Secret Doctrine.

Triad. The Spiritual Man; the expression of the monad. It is the germinal spirit containing the potentialities of divinity. These potentialities will be unfolded during the course of evolution. This Triad forms the individualised or separated self, or Ego.

Viveka. The Sanskrit "discrimination." The very first step in the path of occultism......is the discrimination between the real and the unreal, between substance and phenomenon, between the Self and the Not-self, between spirit and matter.

Wesak. A festival which takes place in the Himalyas at the full moon of May. It is said that at this festival, at which all the members of the Hierarchy are present, the Buddha, for a brief period, renews his touch and association with the work of our planet.

Yoga. 1. One of the six schools of India, said to be founded by Patanjali, but really of much earlier origin. 2. The practice of Meditation as a means of leading to spiritual liberation.

Note: This glossary does not undertake fully to explain all the above terms. It is simply an attempt to render into English certain words used in this book, so that the reader may understand their connotation. The majority of the definitions have been culled from the Theosophical Glossary, The Secret Doctrine, and the Voice of the Silence.

Training for new age

discipleship is provided

by the *Arcane School*.

The principles of the

Ageless Wisdom are

presented through esoteric

meditation, study and

service as a *way of life*.

*Write to the publishers
for information.*

INDEX

A

Absolute, consciousness, 92
Activity, meaning, lesson, 167
Adept, definitions, 179, 180, 198–199, 215
Adepts, work, 90
Adeptship, powers and activities, 89–91
Akashic records—
  care and tabulation, 40
  reading, 170, 172
Alchemy, comprehension, 207
Ancient of Days. *See* Sanat Kumara.
Animal—
  forms, production, 152
  kingdom, door to human, closing, 34
Animal-man, individualisation, 127
Antahkarana—
  definition, 215
  force, 140
  revelation, 173
Applicants for initiation, mark, 108, 183, 192–208
Apollonius of Tyana, initiation, 56–57
Arhat initiation. *See* Initiation, fourth.
Ashram—
  definition, 215
  teaching, 69
Aspect—
  Brahma—
    sacred sound, 153
    secret, initiation, energy, planes, 175
    shining forth, 156
    sphere of endeavour, 171, 172
  destroyer, work and method, 174
  fire, revelation, 174
  first, effects in animal kingdom, 22
  first, mystery, 168
  form-builder—
    body for spirit, 153
    concretising, 3
    effect of Words, 159
  Love-Wisdom, consummation, 22
  second—
    in Hall of Learning, 167
    in vegetable kingdom, 21

Aspect—Continued
  second—Continued
    mystery, 168, 174
    shining forth, 157
  Shiva—
    perfection, 174
    sacred sound, 153
    secret, initiation, energy, planes, 175
  Son, sound, 153
  third—
    electricity, 171
    mystery, 168
    reflection in minerals, 22
    shining forth, 156
  Vishnu—
    domination, 172
    sacred sound, 153
    secret, initiation, energy, planes, 175
    shining forth, 157
  will, forces, 168
  will, sound, 153
Aspirants, meditation, 157
Astral—
  light, mystery, 170
  situation, control, 76–77
Astrological conditions, effect on initiation, 95
Astrology, esoteric and cosmic, use, 143
Atom—
  coherence, 169
  of physics or chemistry, attributes, 159
  opportunity, 162
Atomic—
  matter in bodies, 16, 67
  subplane, definition, 216
  subplane matter, presence, 67
Atoms—
  permanent—
    definition, 222
    manasic, 140
    of Triad, 139
    spirillae, 139
At-one-ment—
  attainment, 18–19
  of Planetary Logos, 172
  processes, 173

227